The Low-Carb Bartender

Carb Counts for Beer, Wine, Mixed Drinks, and More

Bob Skilnik

Author of *The Drink Beer, Get Thin Diet: A Low Carbohydrate Approach*

Adams Media
Avon, Massachusetts

Published by Adams Media, an F+W Publications Company
57 Littlefield Street, Avon, MA 02322 U.S.A.
www.adamsmedia.com

ISBN: 1-59337-253-1

Printed in Canada.

J I H G F E D C B A

Library of Congress Cataloging-in-Publication Data
Skilnik, Bob.
The low-carb bartender / Bob Skilnik.
p.   cm.
ISBN 1-59337-253-1
1. Cocktails. 2. Low-carbohydrate diet–Recipes. I. Title.

TX951.S585 2004
641.8'74–dc22

2004013267

Martini photo ©PhotoDisc. Glass photo ©BananaStock.

The Frenchman loves his native wine;
    The German loves his beer;
The Englishman loves his 'alf and 'alf,
    Because it brings good cheer.
The Irishman loves his "whiskey straight,"
    Because it gives him dizziness;
The American has no choice at all,
    So he drinks the whole damn business.

—Author Unknown
From *The New Bartender's Guide*
Royal Publishing, Baltimore, Maryland, 1914

Contents

Acknowledgments / vii
Preface / xi

1   *The Low-Carb Bartender* / 1

2   Beer, Brewing, and Those Pesky Carbohydrates / 27

3   Carbohydrate Counts of Beer / 39

4   Ale-/Beer-Based Drinks / 83

5   Making *Low-Carb Bartender* Liqueurs and
    Cordials / 95

6   Mixed Drink Recipes Using *Low-Carb Bartender*
    Liqueurs / 125

7   Carbohydrate Counts of Popular Wines, Champagnes,
    Sparkling Wines, and Wine Blends / 135

8   Wine-, Champagne-, and Sparkling Wine-Based
    Drinks / 155

9   Bourbon-Based Drinks / 165

10 Brandy-Based Drinks / 175

11 Frozen/Blender Drinks / 185

12   Gin-Based Drinks / 197

13   Hot Drinks / 207

14   Rum-Based Drinks / 213

15   Tequila-Based Drinks / 223

16   Vodka-Based Drinks / 233

17   Whiskey- (or Whisky-) Based Drinks / 243

18   Martinis / 255

19   FAQs / 267

Appendix A: Bar Measurements / 276

Appendix B: Products and Web Sites / 277

Index / 280

About the Author / 286

Acknowledgments

A reference book like *The Low-Carb Bartender* is a compilation of information provided by many sources. One problem in gathering this information, however, was that a number of representatives of the beer, wine, and spirit industries dismissed the idea of equating their products with what I felt were the desires of carbohydrate-watching customers. On the other hand, some manufacturers of spirited beverages have realized that they have to be responsive to the movements and trends of their markets—even if they might disagree with them.

A common argument that I often used when trying to wrestle information from a wavering industry representative was a simple, but effective one: "Provide me with the carbohydrate information of your products for listing in this book. If your customers watch their carbohydrate intake, give them a reason to continue to enjoy your products—or watch them walk past your beer, wine, or liquor displays at retailers and liquor stores and reach for a bottle from a more cooperative competitor."

The following breweries and brewpubs were extremely helpful in providing information found in this book—Alaskan, Amstel, Anheuser-Busch, Atlanta Brewing, Baltika, Beck's, Bitburger, Bochkarev, Boston Beer Company, Brand, Budweiser Budvar, Caledonian, Carlsberg, Cedar Brewing, Cooper's, the Coors Brewing Company, DB Breweries, Foster's, Goose Island, Grant's, Grolsch, Heineken, Highfalls, Hops Grillhouse & Brewery, Hudepohl-Schoenling, Kona, Leinenkugel, Lion-Nathan, Lost Coast, Miller Brewing Company, Mishawaka, New Belgium, Pabst, Pony Express, Primus, Redhook, Sarapul's, Shipyard, Sierra Nevada, Sinebrychoff, Spoetzl, Straub, Tinkoff, Two Brothers, Widmer Brothers, and Young's.

Other breweries listed in this book provided material specifications of their products either in correspondence to me or via their Web sites. In these cases, carbohydrate counts for their beers were calculated with the help of brewer Mike Snyder from the Cedar Brewing Company in Cedar Rapids, Iowa, and his plug-in formulas for carbohydrate calculations in beer. Mike's efforts were derived from the earlier writings of Doctor Peter Ensminger, who worked with information developed by brewer Jan DeClerck in his *A Textbook of Brewing*, 1957, and "Caloric Content, Beer," an article in the American Society of Brewing Chemists' *Methods of Analysis*, 1992. Ensminger's calculations led to Snyder's JavaScripted tool for carbohydrate, calorie, and alcohol content of beer at *www.mrgoodbeer.com/carb-cal.shtml*.

Lyn Kruger, president of the World Brewing Academy/ Siebel Institute of Technology in Chicago, provided me with the results of a number of lab reports for beers from their analytical lab services department. The Siebel Institute has been turning out new brewers for the brewing industry and adding to the knowledge of seasoned *Braumeisters* from around the world for more than one hundred and twenty-five years. I'm especially fond of this oldest school for brewers in the United States, having received a degree in Brewing Technology from Siebel in 1991.

After hundreds of unanswered letters and e-mails to vintners around the world, I almost gave up on gathering carbohydrate information for wines. I was extremely fortunate, however, to make contact with Sheryl Hoffman at the E. & J. Gallo Winery. Without her help, there might have only been a mere handful of wines listed in this book with their carbohydrate counts. Gallo's wine holdings are much more extensive than years ago, spanning a diverse selection from popular-priced wines to reserve bottlings. Because of Gallo's help, I try to enjoy a Gallo-owned wine product whenever I can—not only because they provided me with information for this book, but also because they offer some fine wines. I strongly suggest you enjoy their products, too.

Tom Scott, Director of Public Relations at the Diageo & Estate Wines Company, came through with carbohydrate counts for many of the firm's French- and American-made wines while this book was going through its final edit. The parent firm of U.K.-based Diageo p.l.c. has recently begun a campaign to eventually list the carbohydrate counts of their adult beverage products sold in North America on their Web site (*www.diageo.com*), promotional literature, and product labels. The listing in *The Low-Carb Bartender* of their wines with carb counts is the first detailed and concise guide ever published. Carb watchers will certainly be impressed with the depth, sophistication, and low-carbohydrate counts of the Diageo & Estate Wines portfolio.

I also raise a glass to Almaden (*www.almaden.com*) and Sutter Home Winery (*www.sutterhome.com*) for providing the nutritional information of their products on their Web sites. It's refreshing to find vintners who understand the increasing demands of their consumers, and make the effort to satisfy those demands.

Thanks also to Katie Felix, Marketing Assistant at Winesellers, Ltd. Until the day this book's manuscript was in the hands of the publisher, Katie continued to try to find at least one vintner in Winesellers's portfolio of fine wines who could provide carbohydrate information of their wines—but to no avail. "Why is it so hard to find the nutritional information?" she once e-mailed me in frustration. Her efforts, however, were appreciated, as were her kind words of encouragement while I wrote *The Low-Carb Bartender*.

A final thanks to my wife Daria, my mother-in-law Sofija Zeimys, and other relatives and friends who willingly participated as guinea pigs for the tasting of a vast majority of the low-carb inspired drink recipes in *The Low-Carb Bartender*. I'm afraid that if this portion of the making of the book had been left to me alone—it might still be a work-in-progress!

Preface

After the success of *The Drink Beer, Get Thin Diet: A Low Carbohydrate Approach* (1st Books, Bloomington, IN, May 2003), it became obvious to me that carb-watching wine and spirit drinkers also needed something to call their own. As I pointed out earlier, all of the low-carb or controlled-carbohydrate diet books on the market today take a cursory and confusing attitude toward enjoying an alcoholic drink or two while counting carbohydrates.

And why is that? The biggest reason, I'm sure, is that the authors of these books really don't know the carbohydrate counts of most beers, wines, and spirits. Rather than dwell on the inclusion of alcoholic drinks in a low-carb diet or controlled-carbohydrate lifestyle, most diet book authors ignore the subject or choose instead to skirt their way around the issue of just how many carbohydrates are in spirited drinks. When I see a popular diet book giving carbohydrate content advice about alcoholic drinks and the word "usually," as in "Red wine usually contains 2 grams of carbohydrates," I know that author is nutritionally shooting from the hip.

There's not a low-carbohydrate diet book on the market today that I don't have stacked in my bookcase. Every one of them, however, fails to realistically address the moderate consumption of alcohol-based beverages, and how to tally up their true carb counts in their low-carbohydrate (LC) diet plans. Having spent considerable time checking numerous sources for nutritional food values for beer, wine, and other spirited drinks while I struggled to lose weight following the guidelines of typical LC diet plans, all I could find were pithy instances of carbohydrate information for alcohol-based drinks. The few wines and beers sometimes referred to in food nutritional value books are often no longer sold or these books list regional beverage brands, isolated in their marketing and distribution. *The Low-Carb Bartender* will make your carbohydrate-watching that much easier.

Check the carbohydrate counts of the beverages listed in this book and you'll note that the word "usually" is nowhere to be found when speaking of alcoholic drinks and carbohydrate counts. If you're like me, you want hard numbers—real carb counts, not generalities—whether you're watching what you eat *or* drink!

This book not only addresses the generalities in carbohydrate counts and alcohol-based beverages—it also clarifies misinformation about alcohol and LC dieting in general, much of which is brought to you by the Internet. Some well-meaning LC Web sites mistakenly try to make a distinction between vodka versus "other grain-based spirits," for instance, the implication being that vodka is made from who knows what—but not grain—and therefore implicitly lower in carbohydrates. The fact that distilled vodka is also grain-based seems to elude those who continue to pass on this incorrect tidbit of information. Check the FAQs in Chapter 19 for a refutation of more LC diet and alcohol related myths.

As one goes through other LC Web sites, beer drinkers seemingly are relegated to drinking "light" or low-carb beers for the rest of their lives, even while in a generous maintenance phase of 60, 70, or even 100 or more carbohydrates a day. A number of popular LC diets even have a problem with maltose, a sugar sometimes found in trace amounts in beer, if at all. The fact that maltose is converted to alcohol and carbon dioxide during fermentation is ignored, leading to the incorrect assumption that maltose remains the major component of beer, even after fermentation. As most knowledgeable beer drinkers might know, water makes up 95 percent of the composition of beer—that's the major component, not maltose! As a beer drinker who has managed to shed over 80 pounds while enjoying moderate amounts of "liquid bread," I'm here to set the record straight—both light and regular-brewed beers can be included in the menu of anyone watching their carb intake. Moderation is the key.

In the United States, alcohol is not considered a food but a controlled substance. As such, its regulation now falls under the auspices of the Alcohol and Tobacco Tax and Trade Bureau (TTB). From 1972 until January 2003, this Department of the Treasury division was called the Bureau of Alcohol, Tobacco and Firearms (ATF). Among other, more obvious measures, the Homeland Security Act separated weapons and crime from the ATF functions.

Responsibility for regulation of firearms and explosives, along with arson and criminal investigations involving alcohol and tobacco, such as smuggling, went to the Justice Department. As with the ATF, the TTB does not require brewers, vintners, or distillers to list any nutritional analyses on their products.

Diageo, one of the world's leading premium drink companies, however, has recently announced that in 2004 it will begin to voluntarily label the nutritional values of all their products to include carbohydrate contents. In late 2003, Ipsos Public Affairs, on behalf of Diageo, stated in a press release that "35 million plus low-carb converts in the U.S. are missing out on the party." The survey found that confusion reigns supreme when it comes to drinking while watching carbs. Their press release caught my eye since I have long been advocating that the typical LC dieter could still lose weight or maintain their weight loss while enjoying the moderate consumption of alcohol. A very savvy Diageo is willing to jump onto the same LC wave that brewers are now riding with their monthly rollout of more new low-carbohydrate beers. Go to *www.lowcarbparties.com* for low-carb drink recipes using Diageo liquors. The times, they are a-changin'.

The Center for Science in the Public Interest and the National Consumers League, two public advocacy groups, also petitioned the TTB in December of 2003 to open up the idea of specific and mandatory labeling requirements on all alcoholic beverages. This would include the concept of what constitutes moderate consumption through suggested serving sizes and the possibility of listing ingredients and nutritional values on all products. As much as I applaud their efforts, I expect a lot of resistance to this.

Since the years immediately following the repeal of National Prohibition in 1933, various departments of the federal government have done everything they could to dissuade the notion that alcohol might be curative, therapeutic, or nutritive. Nutritional labeling, and all that it might imply, will thus most likely be frowned upon.

But as the battle continues between brewers trying to catch the eyes of LC dieters, the TTB has recently loosened up decades of conservative federal rules and regulations that have discouraged the accurate nutritive labeling of all alcohol-based products. They have done so by allowing the manufacturers of adult beverages to *voluntarily* list the calorie and carbohydrate contents of their products. It's only a matter of time, however, before mandatory labeling requirements of all alcohol-based drink products will come into effect, maybe five years or more—but I wouldn't hold my breath on this taking place any earlier. It will nonetheless be interesting to see if other drink manufacturers, aside from Diageo, will follow suit and add calorie and carbohydrate information to their labels.

All the innuendoes, half-truths, and a large helping of misguided "I think," "usually," and "check the label" suggestions for carbohydrate information (when no mandatory nutritive labeling exists on alcohol-based drinks, except light beers and wines) that are floating around the Internet or found in the latest low-carb diet books put LC or controlled-carb individuals in a bit of a quandary. If they want to enjoy a drink or two while following a LC diet or a controlled-carbohydrate lifestyle—and accurately count carbohydrates—what can they do? They could rely on the pithy average nutritional analyses offered by the United States Department of Agriculture (USDA) Web site for beer, wine, and spirits. They would soon discover, however, that it's impossible to get an accurate carb count for the thousands of alcohol-based beverage brands, styles, bottlings, or appellations available today. Use the contents of *The Low-Carb Bartender* to get the real (not average) carbohydrate counts for hundreds of spirited products.

Whether you're on Atkins, South Beach, Protein Power, or your own interpretation of a LC diet, or just following a controlled-carbohydrate lifestyle, there's something in *The Low-Carb Bartender* for you!

I believe that the ultimate goal of anyone following an LC diet should be to evolve their eating and drinking habits into a controlled-carbohydrate regime—to not only lose weight, but to keep it off. That involves a lifestyle change dedicated to moderation in both eating and drinking. It also means that you can live a normal life, eating and drinking virtually anything you want by keeping tabs on your daily carbohydrate intake. The carb counts for alcohol-based beverages listed in this book will make your accountability that much easier.

This book is not for teetotalers or carb-counting fanatics who don't understand that a LC diet, and ultimately a controlled-carbohydrate lifestyle, doesn't mean that eating and drinking should consist of months of endless suffering and remorse. If you're also going to argue that drinking alcohol slows down one's weight loss or that booze is nothing more than "empty carbs," put down this book. *The Low-Carb Bartender* is for LC dieters who want to have a choice, whether they decide to enjoy a drink or two with their meals or at a social occasion—or not. But as you'll read, I'm also not advocating swilling down a quart of vodka this weekend or belching one's way through a twelve-pack of beer tonight. The inconsequential slowdown of weight caused by enjoying one or two drinks with a meal or snack is worth the price, I think, for a few moments of rest and reflection while enjoying a beer, wine, or mixed drink. If you have read this far through the preface of this book, I suspect that you share my sentiments.

Consider the fact that by carefully monitoring your eating and drinking habits, you will be training yourself to reach your ultimate goal of weight loss with a steady, consistent return to an ideal weight, not the yo-yo lose-and-gain pattern that you've probably subjected yourself to for years. Most enjoyably, you will achieve this goal through the practice of moderation, not deprivation—and with a drink in your hand!

Cheers!
Bob Skilnik

1

The Low-Carb Bartender

ONE OF THE MOST COMMON ARGUMENTS VOICED by critics is that low-carbohydrate diets are often dull and uninspiring in their choices of allowable foods. "That's the diet where all you do is eat meat," says one. "I'd get tired of eating bacon and eggs every day," says another naysayer. Of course, they've probably never picked up a low-carb diet book in their lives. Their perceptions of LCing are usually gleaned from the media. How many times have you read a newspaper article or watched the news on TV and heard a reporter label low-carb diets as "high protein" or "high fat," or even worse, "no carbs"? Talk about misinformation.

Unfortunately, there are times when these same concepts and complaints come from the mouths of LC dieters themselves. "I'm so tired of eating meat all the time!" or "If I eat bacon and eggs one more time for breakfast, I'm going to scream!"

I can almost absolve the media for their false perceptions of LC diets. Their job is to catch your eye or hold your attention for a minute or two. Sensationalism sells the story. A buzzword or a catch phrase here or there can make you sit up and take notice. I can't, however, excuse LC dieters who complain that a low-carbohydrate diet regime is dull, dull, dull. In *The Drink Beer, Get Thin Diet: A Low Carbohydrate Approach*, I stressed the ideas of variety in the diet and the absolute need for planning and preparation when beginning a LC weight-loss program. I know it can be the easiest thing to do to come home after a long day at work, fry up a frozen hamburger patty or two, heat a can of green beans, and make a simple salad of head lettuce. It's easy—and dull—and can be the eventual pathway to boredom and weight-loss failure.

Planning, preparation, and variety are the keys to LC success. Whether it's with food or drink, a well-stocked pantry, freezer, and bar can go a long way in keeping you on track. With this thought in mind, and keeping with the theme of this book, let's begin by putting together suggested ingredients and accessories needed by anyone who wants to become a *Low-Carb Bartender*, a concept that embraces both the low- and controlled-carbohydrate lifestyles. The concept is a fluid one (no pun intended), depending more on your likes and dislikes, space consideration, and what beverages you actually have on hand. Use this information as a guide, not as a mandate.

The Usual Suspects

Drinking while LCing can be a perfunctory exercise of simply opening up a bottle of beer or a jug of wine or pouring a shot of whiskey into a glass of diet ginger ale. It can also be an accompaniment to the lingering pleasure of mulling over the day's events with friends or family. At times, drinking can even be ritualistic, hoisting a glass for a toast during a wedding or to remember those who are no longer with us or those who are soon to return.

Take pleasure in a glass or two of whatever you're drinking, and whenever. With something as simple as choosing the proper glass for your drink, to having an assortment of key ingredients and equipment readily available in your bar, planning ahead will add to the pleasures of a drink and add variety to any LC lifestyle.

Bar Stock and Supplies

As a *Low-Carb Bartender*, you'll be facing the challenges of assembling and preparing all the necessities for pleasing yourself and your guests with great tasting drinks, especially if some of your drinking companions aren't counting carbs. It will make your tasks that much simpler if all your tools and ingredients are readily available.

Barware

If you're going to incorporate the moderate consumption of alcohol-based drinks into your menu while following a LC diet or controlled-carbohydrate lifestyle, the following suggested implements should be kept on hand by any *Low-Carb Bartender*.

Blender

Into blended drinks? Make the initial purchase of one with a heavy motor. If you cheap out and buy one of those plastic jobs, the motor will inevitably burn out while valiantly trying to cut down rock-hard ice cubes. Who wants to be hosting a summertime party when the blender goes dead?

Bottle/Can Opener

Not all beers have twist-off caps. Quart-sized tomato juice cans almost always need to be opened with a can opener, so keep a dual purpose "church key" on hand. You might already have one buried in the back of a kitchen drawer.

Corkscrew/Wine Opener

Once again, go cheap and it will fall apart when you need it most. The Rabbit Corkscrew by Metrokane is a high-end cork-puller that does the job in a most efficient way.

Cutting Board

You'll need a small, plastic board, nothing fancy. Use for slicing up garnishes like lemons and limes.

Grater

A small, hand-held one is fine. Use often to grate a sprinkle or two of fresh nutmeg topping on creamed drinks.

Ice Bucket/Tongs

Buy a good-sized insulated bucket so you don't have to keep on running back to the freezer. Tongs normally come with the bucket.

Knife

A small, serrated one works best for cutting up lemons and limes, but a sharp knife will do a better job when making lemon or lime twists. Get one of each.

Measuring/Shot Glass

Get the double-ended stainless steel one with a 1-ounce "pony" measure on one side, and a 1½-ounce "jigger" on the other.

Mixing Sticks

Aside from their obvious use, they do add a decorative touch to a drink.

Napkins

Serve one with each drink and that will be one less bottle or glass water ring you'll have to clean up from your end tables the day after your next party.

Pepper Mill

A nice touch when topping off a drink like a Bloody Mary with some pepper. You might also have one of these in the kitchen or pantry.

Reamer

If you're going to go through a lot of lemons and limes for juicing, a cheap wooden one will speed up the process and extract more juice than just squeezing them by hand. Use this over a small bowl while extracting juice so you don't also serve your next mixed drink with seeds as an unintended garnish!

Shaker

Although the three-piece cocktail shaker/strainer combo with rounded lid seems quite convenient, I sometimes have problems with the strainer clogging up. I much prefer the traditional two-piece Boston shaker with a separate strainer. This consists of separate glass and metal containers, one cupped into the other while shaking up a drink. The glass portion can also do double-duty as a mixing glass. Grasping the container and pouring out a drink while looping a finger over the strainer to keep it in place is an acquired art, but not rocket science.

Spoon

A long bar spoon is advisable, especially when you're digging for that last olive in the jar or stirring a pitcher of dry martinis, but you could probably get away with something found in your everyday silverware drawer, too.

Beer/Ale

If you're entertaining, remember that not all your guests think like you or watch their carbohydrate intake. Always keep some low-carb *and* regular-brewed beers on hand. Check the extensive list of beers with their carbohydrate counts in this book for your best choices.

Dairy

Whipping cream, heavy cream, or half-and-half are traditionally called for in many cream-based drinks such as a White Russian. Although 1 ounce of cream runs about 1 carbohydrate and should be used somewhat sparingly if you're concerned about saturated fat, H.P. Hood & Sons of Chelsea, Mass, has recently come out with Carb Countdown—actual milk that has the sugar removed from it. At only 3 carbohydrates per 8-ounce serving, their homogenized, 2% reduced fat, and fat-free brands can be substituted, if desired, for heavy or whipping cream in mixed drinks. Hood's Carb Countdown 2% Reduced Fat Chocolate Dairy Beverage also boasts 3 carbs per 8-ounce serving plus 1 gram of fiber for a net carb count of 2 grams per serving. At the moment, the dairy beverage only comes in half-gallon containers. All Carb Countdown products are Atkins-approved.

Garnishes

A nice touch like a maraschino cherry makes a colorful drink garnish, but a momentary lapse could turn a few of these into high-carb bombs. To keep the carb counts down, stay with the following *Low-Carb Bartender* garnishes:

- Celery sticks
- Cocktail onions
- Dill pickle spears
- Green cocktail olives (stuffed or otherwise)
- Green onions
- Lemons
- Limes
- Mint leaves
- Oranges (thin-sliced)
- Strawberries

Remember, they're not called "garnishes" for nothing. They add flair to a drink presentation, but that doesn't mean you have to eat every garnish served with your drink.

Glasses

Please—no canning or jelly jars here! You're trying to do whatever you can to beat the boredom that might creep into any LC diet or controlled-carbohydrate lifestyle, just as you would when planning a food menu or preparing a meal. Remember that it's the little things that can put a refreshing spin on something as simple as a can of beer or a serving from a cheaper box of wine.

Beer mug or stein: Usually a thick glass with handle—16 ounces

Brandy snifter: Small-stemmed, balloon-shaped glass—5 to 25 ounces

Champagne flute: Tall, thin glass for champagne or sparkling wine—6 to 10 ounces

Cocktail glass: Also known as a martini glass—4 to 6 ounces

Collins glass: Tall, skinny glass, sometimes frosted—10 to 16 ounces

Cordial glass: Small-stemmed glass for liqueurs or apéritifs—2 ounces

Coupette glass: More commonly known as a margarita glass—12 ounces

English pint glass: Can do double duty as an appropriate container for beer or ale, especially from the tap, or as a mixing glass—14 to 16 ounces

Highball glass: Same diameter from bottom to top—12 ounces

Hurricane glass: Tall, balloon-shaped glass—16 ounces

Irish coffee goblet: Short-stemmed, clear mug with handle—8 to 10 ounces

Old-fashioned glass: Same diameter from bottom to top—4 to 8 ounces

Pilsner glass: V-shaped, small-stemmed beer glass—12 to 16 ounces

Red wine glass: Long-stemmed, bulbous glass—8 to 10 ounces

Shot glass: Or as we call them in Chicago, a shooter. As a bar essential, you might be better off with a two-ended metal shot glass that can hold 1 ounce (a "pony") on one end and 1½ ounces (a "jigger") on the other end. A shot glass, however, is a key component in some drinks such as a Depth Charge.

Whiskey sour glass: Similar in appearance to a champagne flute—5 ounces

White wine glass: Smaller and not quite as elegant as the larger red wine glass. Most people don't know the difference between a red wine glass and a white wine glass so you could probably get away with just one type of wine glass in your bar—6 to 8 ounces

Ice

Used in almost all mixed drinks. Just remember to toss old ice from a finished drink. That's right—use new ice for each serving rather than a combination of fresh ingredients and diluted "bad bottoms."

Liqueurs/Cordials

As a LC dieter, you might consider the liqueur category of alcohol-based drinks a scary one. Liqueurs contain at least two-and-one-half percent sugar in order to be considered a liqueur, but more often than not, these concoctions will actually consist of 30 to 40 percent sugar. I present the list below merely as very guarded suggestions.

The taste and color of liqueurs is a result of the maceration, infusion, percolation, or distillation of plants' leaves, seeds, or roots, or fruits or herbs to spice up the liquid.

Depending on what stage of a LC diet you're on, including any form of weight maintenance, the judicious use of these products is strongly advised. Personally, I would avoid them—but this book is about choices. There is a section later in the book, however, that shows you how to make *Low-Carb Bartender (LCB)* versions of a number of these items at home, an option that opens up hundreds of new drink ideas for anyone watching their carbohydrate intake.

While you might not have the space to keep the following liqueurs on hand, there is one in particular that you'll find indispensable. Grand Marnier, even with its 6.5 carbs per 1-ounce serving, it can be used in any mixed drink recipe that calls for Triple Sec, Cointreau, and of course, Grand Marnier. Its lower carbohydrate count, as compared to other liqueurs, makes it a number one "must have" real liqueur.

Amaretto

An Italian liqueur made from apricot stones but with a strong smell of almonds. Extremely sweet and has a slight syrupy viscosity because of the high sugar content.

Benedictine

A French liqueur that was actually used in the 1500s to combat malaria. Flavors of honey, citrus, and herbs such as rosemary, basil, and sage. Mix it half and half with brandy, preferably a good French brandy, and you now have a B & B (Benedictine & Brandy) at only 2.5 carbs per 1-ounce serving.

Chambord

A black raspberry liqueur from France. Serve it on the rocks or as an added splash in champagne.

Crème de Menthe (clear or green)

If I do buy this liqueur, I usually get the green version figuring if it tastes like mint, it should look like mint, too! The use of the word "crème" in any liqueur indicates a somewhat sweeter than usual taste, though it does not actually have cream in it. I actually prefer peppermint schnapps as a lower-carbohydrate alternative to Crème de Menthe, green or clear.

Grand Marnier

Actually a high-priced Triple Sec, but in my opinion, worth every penny. A French product made with cognac, essence of wild oranges, and delicate syrup. The mixture is aged in oak casks prior to bottling. A key ingredient, I think, in a real margarita.

Irish Cream

Rich in cream and eggs, it has a taste and aroma of honey, cream, and cocoa. It's easy to get carried away with this drink—too easy—so be careful.

Kahlúa

America's number-one imported liqueur. It has a rich brown color and aromas of coffee beans with earthy flavors of coffee and semisweet chocolate. Mixed with heavy cream and vodka, it makes a great White Russian. To keep my liqueur collection reasonably sized, I use Kahlúa in recipes that also call for Crème de Cacao for my nonLCing friends.

Peppermint Schnapps

As explained above, peppermint schnapps is a lower-carb alternative to Crème de Menthe, though a tad bit stronger in mint flavor.

Sambuca (Clear or Black)

I hate the taste of black licorice but love Sambuca. Go figure. To me, the dark version actually tastes smoother than the clear product. The idea of sitting back with a cordial or two on a LC diet might hit a hot button with some of you—and it should. In the interest of making this book all things for all LC people, you will find a number of *Low-Carb Bartender* options in Chapter 4 that might have you enjoying—without guilt—the perilous path that sugar-laden liqueurs can lead you down. With the observation that most liqueurs are composed of a high percentage of sugar, I began to toy around with the idea of formulating my own *Low-Carb Bartender* (*LCB*) liqueurs using Splenda as a substitute for sugar. Little did I know that there is a whole world of liqueur recipes and essences available that can be reformulated into enjoyable *LCB* liqueur products.

Liqueurs

Call them liqueurs or cordials. Just remember that these liquor-based sweetened drinks should be avoided by LC dieters or judiciously enjoyed on rare occasions by anyone simply watching their carb intake.

You'll notice that some of the following liqueurs seem to fall into an average carbohydrate range of around 11 grams in a 1-ounce serving. Many liqueurs have an alcoholic strength of about 50° to 60° proof, or 25% to 30% alcohol. The rest of the product consists of a small percentage of the herb, plant, or fruit base—and the rest of sugar syrup or even honey. This average alcohol/sugar syrup ratio leads to many of the products below being similar in carbohydrate composition.

Liqueurs

99 Bananas Schnapps	1 oz	8.1 g
Aftershock	1 oz	11 g
Alize	1 oz	11 g
Amaretto Di Saronno	1 oz	17 g
Archers Peach Schnapps	1 oz	6.6 g
Arrow Peach Schnapps	1 oz	6.6 g
Avalanche Peppermint Schnapps	1 oz	7.4 g
Bandolero Triple Sec	1 oz	11 g
Becherovka	1 oz	11 g
Benedictine	1 oz	5 g
Berentzen's Apple Liqueur	1 oz	11 g
Blue Curaçao	1 oz	7 g
Blue Tattoo Blueberry Schnapps	1 oz	10.6 g
Bols Blue Curaçao	1 oz	7 g
Chambord	1 oz	11 g
Cherry Brandy	1 oz	9 g
Chymos Cranberry Liqueur	1 oz	11 g
Coffee with Cream (Baileys)	1 oz	6 g
Cointreau	1 oz	7 g
Continental Cherry Advocaat	1 oz	9 g
Crème de Bananes	1 oz	11 g
Crème de Cacao	1 oz	15 g
Crème de Cassis	1 oz	11 g
DeKuyper Sour Apple Pucker	1 oz	8.1 g
Deva Absinthe	1 oz	11 g
Dr. McGillicuddy's Vanilla Schnapps	1 oz	8.1 g
Drambuie	1 oz	9 g
Droste Chocolate Liqueur	1 oz	11 g
Frangelico Hazelnut Liqueur	1 oz	11 g
Galliano	1 oz	11 g
Godet White Chocolate	1 oz	11 g

Liqueurs (continued)

Godiva	1 oz	11 g
Goldschlager	1 oz	11 g
Grand Marnier	1 oz	6.5 g
Greizer Strawberry Liqueur	1 oz	11 g
Hiram Walker Blue Curaçao	1 oz	7 g
Jacquin's Crème de Fraise	1 oz	11 g
Jaegermeister	1 oz	11 g
Jubilee Peach Schnapps	1 oz	6.6 g
Kamora Coffee Liqueur	1 oz	11 g
Kirsch	1 oz	6 g
Lapponia Lakka Cloudberry	1 oz	11 g
Liqueur, Coffee (Kahlúa)	1 oz	11 g
Luxardo Limoncello	1 oz	11 g
Mari Mayans Absinthe	1 oz	11 g
Marie Brizard Mango Passion	1 oz	11 g
Maui Tropical Schnapps	1 oz	10.6 g
McGuinness Crème de Menthe	1 oz	14 g
Midori	1 oz	11 g
Opal Nera Black Sambuca	1 oz	11 g
Original Mozart Chocolate	1 oz	11 g
Pernod	1 oz	11 g
Phillips Raspberry Schnapps	1 oz	10.6 g
Romano Sambuca	1 oz	11 g
Rumple Minze Peppermint	1 oz	7.4 g
Saurer Apfel Apple Schnapps	1 oz	8.1 g
St. Halivard	1 oz	11 g
Tia Maria	1 oz	10 g
Tortuga Rum Cream	1 oz	11 g
Triple Sec	1 oz	11 g
Truffles Chocolate	1 oz	11 g
Yukon Jack	1 oz	11 g

Liquors

Distilled products make great choices for anyone who wants to enjoy the relaxing pleasures of a drink or two while counting carbs. In general, high-potency liquors are carb free. Just remember to check the labels for hidden carbohydrates in any mixes you might use in your drinks or as a wash.

Bourbon/Scotch/Whiskey
1 ounce equals < 1 carbohydrate

I know there are purists out there who will strongly disagree with my lumping these three spirits into one group, especially since I have actually broken up LC drink recipes for bourbon, Scotch, and whiskey into separate categories later in the book. Bear with me, however, while I try to save you space and money in building your bar.

Cognac/Brandy
1 ounce of brandy/cognac equals < 1.00–4 carbohydrates

Once again, these are interchangeable spirits, distilled from wine. True cognac, of course, is the finest quality brandy from the Cognac region in France (and more expensive than your standard brandy). Remember, cognac is a brandy, but brandy isn't necessarily a cognac. If you're on a budget, go with brandy. Both of these distilled wines can pick up a small amount of carbohydrates leeched from the tannins and sugars in the wood cells of oak barrels. As the spirit ages and mellows, evaporation can cause the miniscule carb count to increase proportionally as the volume of the brandy or cognac decreases.

The folks at E. & J. Gallo Winery have offered the following carb counts of their brandy and cognac products. Their Cask & Cream brand, in both chocolate and caramel flavors, is actually a brandy liqueur blended with imported cream, which partially accounts for its 8 grams of carbohydrates in a 1-ounce serving. Their Patriarch brandy is aged for twenty years in oak barrels. As mentioned above, tannins, sugars in wood cells, and evaporation account for the concentration of 4 carbs in a 1-ounce serving of Patriarch. One taste, however, and you might find those few carbs are well worth it! Remember, moderation—not deprivation!

E. & J. Gallo Brandies, Cognac

Brandy	I oz	0 g
VSOP Brandy	I oz	1.2 g
White Brandy	I oz	0 g
Cask & Cream	I oz	8 g
Patriarch	I oz	4 g
Cognac	I oz	1.2 g

The lighter the color, the less carbs. If ever in doubt about the carb count of any brandy or cognac, choose a clear product, always around zero carbohydrates.

Gin
1 ounce equals < 1 carbohydrate

Look for any gin described as "London Dry." Geneva (or Genever), sometimes even called Holland gin, can also be used, but it has a taste similar to Scotch, a result of its unique distillation. Avoid any gin labeled as "Old Tom." It is a sweetened gin, thought to be the original gin used in making a Tom Collins.

Rum (Clear and Dark)
1 ounce equals < 1 carbohydrate

Rum is made from the runnings of raw sugar cane or molasses, fermented and then distilled. Light-colored rums are indicative of young rum, usually aged no more than one year. Amber or dark rums usually take on their characteristic colors due to oak barrel aging, though some young rums get a dosing of caramel coloring. Light Puerto Rican rums are almost vodka-like in taste. Jamaican rums are aged and can be topped off with caramel coloring before being bottled. It's customary to use the darker rums in tropical drinks such as a Zombie.

"Coconut-flavored" or "spiced" rums often have sweeteners added to them. Unless you know the carb counts of these rums, avoid them. Here are Captain Morgan's carbohydrate numbers for their flavored and spiced rums.

Captain Morgan Spiced Rums

Original Spiced Rum	1 oz	3.2 g
Silver Spiced Rum	1 oz	1.6 g
Parrot Bay	1 oz	6.24 g
Private Stock	1 oz	2.16 g

Tequila (Clear, Gold, *Reposado*, and *Anejo*)
1 ounce equals < 1 carbohydrate

Tequila is another nongrain-based spirit. Its fermentable base originates from the sweet sap of the blue agave plant. As with rum, tequila picks up its range of light to dark color as a result of aging. A tequila with no aging is sometimes called white or silver tequila. There is gold tequila (usually young white tequila with caramel coloring), amber *reposado* (aged in oak barrels for less than a year), and the even darker *anejo*. With age comes enhanced smoothness and drinkability. The Spanish word *anejo* indicates a quality, aged tequila that has been barreled for more than one year.

Vodka

Vodka is predominately a grain-based spirit made from just about anything and everything, including the addition of potatoes and even molasses in the grain bill of some vodkas. Flavored vodkas such as those from Absolut, Smirnoff, Stolichnaya, Grey Goose, Van Gogh, Fleischmann, and Gordon's are produced without sugar and have zero carbs. The flavored-vodka category has grown over 125 percent in the last few years so it's impossible to keep track of all of them. Stick with the established brands listed above and you'll be okay.

Mixers

For any premade or packaged ingredient, it's important to read the nutritional labels on them. Manufacturers sometimes veer away slightly from standard formulas in order to put their own spin of "uniqueness" on them.

Baja Bob

These premade mixes and dried powders are the only commercial attempts that I am aware of that follow *The Low-Carb Bartender* philosophy—and taste good to boot. The product line ranges from a piña colada mix and various margarita mixes and powders to a new line of Soy Munchables with flavors such as Herb & Garlic and Jalapeno.

Carbohydrate counts for Baja Bob products vary. Check the product labels.

Diet Snapple

With nine different choices of diet drinks, including intriguing selections such as Diet Lime Green Tea and Diet Orange Carrot, these low-carb beverages work well as a mix with any distilled product.

Carbohydrate counts for Diet Snapple products vary from 1 to 4 carbohydrates per serving. Check the product labels.

Fresh Lemon/Lime Juice
1 tablespoon equals 1.00 carbohydrates

Sure, the bottled stuff is more convenient, but the addition of the juice of either one of these fresh citrus fruits will make a world of difference in your drinks. If you're going to use the bottled versions, check their labels. Some of the brands are ever-so-slightly higher in carbohydrates than fresh lemon or lime juice. The added bonus with these fruits is that you can also use the squeezed-out empty shell, wedges, slices, or even the zest of them for drink garnishes. One lemon or lime equals between 2 to 3 tablespoons of juice. Your mileage may vary.

Diet V8 Splash
8 ounces equals 3 carbohydrates

This product by Campbell is a boon for anyone watching carbs and is a good base for lots of great LC mixed drinks, including a New Orleans-style Hurricane. So far, three low-carb flavors are available—Strawberry Kiwi, Berry Blend, and Tropical Blend. At 3 carbs per 8-ounce serving, there's a whole world of tropical or slushy blender drinks that can be made with these flavors. I especially like the Berry Blend in Hurricanes. Get all three and experiment—I think you'll like the *LCB* results!

Ocean Spray Light Juice Drinks
8 ounces equals 10 carbohydrates
These products by Ocean Spray are another lower-carb alternative to traditional fruit-based juices. Flavors are Light Cranberry, Light Cran • Grape, Light Cran • Raspberry, Light White Cranberry, and Light Ruby Grapefruit. These flavors can be worked into a number of *LCB* mixed drinks.

Old Orchard LoCarb Juice Cocktails
8 ounces equals 6 carbohydrates
Actually lower in carbohydrates per serving than the Ocean Spray products, this Splenda-sweetened product is slightly more tart in flavor. Flavors are Apple, Apple Kiwi Strawberry, Apple Cranberry, Apple Raspberry, and Grape.

Sodas and Seltzers
Check labels for exact carbohydrate counts
These include: diet cola, diet lemon-lime, diet lemonade, diet ginger ale, diet tonic, seltzer, soda water, and any other low-carbohydrate carbonated beverage that might be on store shelves today.

Vegetable Juices
8 ounces equals 6–8 carbohydrates; check labels for exact carbohydrate counts
These consist of tomato juice and tomato/vegetable juice.

Seasonings

In the same way that we spice up our foods with the addition of seasonings like common table salt or pepper, a pinch here or a dash there can bring zip and added dimension to most any mixed drink.

Bitters
1/2 teaspoon equals 2 carbohydrates
I use Angostura, made from a secret blend of herbs and spices since 1824.

Black Pepper
1/2 teaspoon equals < 1 carbohydrate
Cracked with a small pepper mill is best, but crushed pepper works fine, too.

Celery Salt
1/2 teaspoon equals < 1 carbohydrate
A key ingredient in a good Bloody Mary.

Nutmeg
1/2 teaspoon equals < 1 carbohydrate
Use a whole piece, grated as needed. The ground and powdered version works well but the whole piece of nutmeg retains a fresher flavor.

Salt
1/2 teaspoon equals < 1 carbohydrate
The type of salt you use is your choice; you may also consider seasoned salt.

Tabasco Sauce
¹/₂ teaspoon equals < 1 carbohydrate

Use McIlhenny Co.—another one of those old family recipes. Made with select peppers and salt, the mash is fermented for three years and then blended with vinegar. Been around since 1868. Hands down, it's the best.

Worcestershire Sauce
¹/₂ teaspoon equals < 1 carbohydrate

Lea & Perrins, like Tabasco, is another one of those "secret" recipe products. Commercially produced since 1837.

Orange Bitters, à la The Low-Carb Bartender

Yields about 1 cup of orange bitters.

A dash or two equals < 1 carbohydrate

These are sometimes hard to find. As far as I can tell, it's only made or imported into the United States by a company called Fee Brothers in Rochester, New York. If you can't find orange bitters, no problem. You can make a *LCB* version.

¹/₄ pound dried orange peels
8 oz grain alcohol (190-proof)
2 tablespoons Splenda
1 pinch cardamom
1 pinch caraway
1 pinch coriander

Put all the ingredients except Splenda into a quart-sized glass canning jar. Put on the lid and tighten.

Shake jar gently for 10 seconds once a day, every day for 3 weeks. After 3 weeks, strain the mixture through a colander lined with cheesecloth.

Pour the liquid back into the canning jar. Put the strained residue into a saucepan and smash the seeds with a spoon.

Pour in boiling water, just enough to cover the seeds and orange peel remains. Put this mixture into a separate small canning jar. Seal and shake.

After 2 days, using a funnel lined with cheesecloth, strain the liquid from the seed/peel runnings into the original mixture in the quart-sized canning jar. Add 2 tablespoons of Splenda to the liquid mixture. Shake again and let it sit for 1 more week.

Strain the *LCB* orange bitters again into a new container using a funnel and conical coffee filter to clarify. Pour the *LCB* orange bitters into a plastic squeeze bottle and refrigerate.

Sweeteners

Shot-and-a-beer old-timers blamed National Prohibition and the hot taste of rotgut booze for the onslaught of sweetened drinks that originated during the Roaring Twenties. The trend nonetheless continues. Satisfying the sweet tooth of LC dieters who crave sweetness in their drinks but not its sugary consequences is easy with the products listed below.

Da Vinci Sugar Free Syrups

The depth of this line of sugar-free (Splenda) flavored syrups is amazing. At last count, there were 45 sugar-free varieties. With flavors such as cherry, cookie dough, eggnog, watermelon, and green apple, the permutations of mixed drinks that can be made with these products is endless. Use your imagination and experiment with this extensive product line. Flavored martinis are extremely easy to make with these syrups by simply adding 1 teaspoon or so to 1½ ounces of vodka or gin. If you go to the Da Vinci Gourmet Web site at *www.davincigourmet.com*, you'll find more than 70 mixed drink recipe ideas, many alcohol-free, which can be tweaked with the addition of your favorite spirits.

Grenadine, à la *The Low-Carb Bartender*
½ teaspoon equals < 1 carbohydrate

What most drinkers don't realize is that true grenadine, prepared from the juice of the red flesh surrounding the seeds of the pomegranate fruit, is mostly a thing of the past. The store-bought grenadine you find on shelves today is often nothing more than sugar or high-fructose corn syrup mixed with water and food coloring. Follow the *LCB* recipe for simple sugar below and either add a drop or two of red food coloring to the syrupy results after boiling, or add a pinch of red-colored Kool-Aid to the Splenda/water solution while it boils down. Grenadine syrup is used more as a color enhancement in a mixed drink than as a flavoring—think Tequila Sunrise, for instance.

Rose's Lime Juice
½ teaspoon equals 1 carbohydrate

Indispensable in so many mixed drinks. Its carb count is low enough to work with, so there is no need to substitute.

Simple Syrup, à la *The Low-Carb Bartender*
½ teaspoon equals < 1 carbohydrate

This is called for in a number of mixed drink recipes, and is normally a combination of cane sugar and water.

For our purposes, mix 2 cups of distilled water to 1 cup of Splenda (or use a ratio of 2 parts distilled water to 1 part Splenda) and boil for 5 to 10 minutes or until the solution starts to thicken slightly. Let it cool and it will actually thicken even more. Aim for a resultant 8 ounces or so. Pour into a new plastic squeeze container, such as what you might find mustard or ketchup in at a greasy spoon. I use a clear one so I don't wind up mistakenly squirting mustard into someone's drink. The unused portion will last indefinitely in the refrigerator but will need a shake or two before using.

Splenda

The argument with a number of LC dieters as to whether this brand-name sugar substitute (sucralose), like any of the others on the market today, will cause adverse physical reactions, slow down weight loss, or cause hair to grow between your knuckles, ranks right up there with other "favorite" barroom arguments like politics and religion. It is useful, however, especially in lieu of the often called-for powdered sugar in some traditional mixed drinks. Splenda is blended with dextrose and maltodextrin in order to add measurability to the sweetener, and as such, contains 24 carbohydrates in a measured 8-ounce cup. The maltodextrin and dextrose blends nicely with liquid.

Could you replace Splenda with other sugar substitutes and save some carbs? Sure, but you may pick up an odd "taste" in most other non-nutritive sweeteners. You might, however, find the alternatives to Splenda more appealing.

Sweet and Sour Mix
¹/₂ teaspoon equals < 1 carbohydrate

Baja Bob's Loco Lemon Sugar Free Sweet-n-Sour Mix is the easiest way to go for an instant sweet/sour addition to a drink. At a little less than 1 carbohydrate per 4-ounce serving, it's a great addition to your bar. Sweet and sour mix is called for in scores of traditional mixed drink recipes.

Want to make your own sweet and sour mix? Take *The Low-Carb Bartender* recipe for simple syrup above and add in ¹/₄ cup of fresh lime juice and ¹/₄ cup of fresh lemon juice to the cooled *LCB* simple syrup. Stir. Pour into a plastic squeeze bottle and refrigerate. Shake before using.

Wines

As with your available beer selection, you may want to mix up your *Low-Carb Bartender* wine inventory, too. Include at least a red and a white, champagne or sparkling wine, and a bottle each of sweet and dry vermouth. Check the carbohydrate list of wines in this book for hundreds of choices.

2

Beer, Brewing, and Those Pesky Carbohydrates

THE ARGUMENT AS TO HOW A *Low-Carb Bartender* customer can enjoy light and regular-brewed beers is covered in detail in *The Drink Beer, Get Thin Diet: A Low Carbohydrate Approach.* Look at counting carbs as simply a numbers game—and as long as you know the carb counts of beer—you'll have room to maneuver through hundreds of them, including regular-brewed brands and the always reliable light and low-carb beers.

Before going to the extensive list of worldwide beers and their carb counts in the next chapter, let's walk through parts of the brewing cycle. Be aware that the following discussion is a generalized one. Breweries often have their own proprietary techniques in making beer.

Carbohydrates in Beer

In order for yeast to transform various simple sugars into alcohol and carbon dioxide, the starches found in malted barley and adjuncts such as corn or rice must be converted from starch to sugar. Before this miracle happens, the barley must be malted. Malted barley is the result of soaking barley in water, letting the grains absorb the water, spreading the water-soaked barley on a cement floor, and allowing it to sprout. As the barley begins to naturally grow and reproduce, enzymes form to convert starches to sugars and amino acids that will supply food for the embryonic acrospire, the beginning of life in the barley.

Before the poor acrospire can bloom into a new barley plant, the barely-growing barley is brought to a kiln—nothing more than a huge oven. The purpose of this step is to end the growing of the seed grain, and stop and seal in the enzymes before they can use up any more starchy food materials in the barley. Depending on how long the barley is heated for or how high of a temperature the kiln is brought to, the color of the barley will turn into a very slight, almost indiscernible shade of golden brown to a dark, roasted coffee-like brown/black appearance. At the darker end of the color spectrum, the sugar-converting enzymes in the barley are destroyed but this darker-colored barley will serve as the coloring agent for various styles of beer, including darker beers like porters or stouts. Most of the barley, however, is lightly kilned, assuring the integrity of the vital enzymes.

What's the purpose of these enzymes? After the dried, now malted barley is crushed to expose the starchy interior of the grain, it is poured, or mashed-in, into heated water. It's at this point in the brewing cycle that the reawakened enzymes get to go to work again. Proteins are broken down in the mash to add richness and mouth-feel in beer. Most important, starches in the malted barley are broken down by these robust enzymes into unfermentable and fermentable sugars, the latter a key to the production of alcohol, the former holding carbohydrates.

At a point determined by the brewer and the style of beer he wants to create, the temperature of this sugary mash is elevated, killing off the thankless enzymes. What's left behind are complex sugars and the fermentable simple sugars.

Light or Lite Beer

Traditionally, if a brewer wanted to make a beer with less sugars left behind, in other words, the beginnings of a "light" beer, a special enzyme (for you technical types—a fungal alpha amylase that changes unfermentable complex sugars called dextrins into fermentable sugars) is normally added to the mash. Remember—it's the simple sugars that yeasts like best. Lately, however, some patient brewers have taken to lengthening the mash cycle to up to six hours, another way of getting most of the complex sugars to eventually break down into fermentable simple ones. Once these dextrins have broken down into simple sugars, yeast is pitched into the cooled wort, or unfermented beer, where it does its job of converting the sugars into alcohol and carbon dioxide.

The end result, whether adding new enzymes into the mash for sugar conversion or extending the mash to utilize the natural enzymes found in the malted barley, is a beer with little residual sugar and high alcohol content.

At this point the alcohol level of the beer has to be brought down to an acceptable range, and with it, resultant lower carbohydrates and calories. This step is usually done by blending filtered and carbonated water into the beer—and this is where the difference between a light beer of only 2.5, 5.0, or 11.70 carbs can occur. Although many of the residual sugars in the wort have been attacked by yeast cells, there are still a number of the more complex dextrinous sugars left behind that have defied the long mashing cycle or the added dose of fungal alpha amylase. By blending water into the beer, a dilution takes place that controls how many carbohydrates and calories per serving will be available, along with bringing down the alcohol content of the brew. Although some light or low-carb beers have about the same alcohol strength as regular-brewed beers, the majority of them are somewhat lower in alcohol content. Alcohol figures predominately in the calorie content of beer. Brewers seem to want to underscore the 100-calories-per-serving level, satisfying those dieters who are watching carbs *and* calories. Less alcohol equals less calories.

Regular-Brewed Beer

With regular-brewed beer, a time frame of about 1 to 2 hours takes place during the mash cycle in order to convert starches to sugars. When the brewer ends the mashing of the malted barley by elevating the temperature of the slurry of sweet water and spent malted barley, complex and simple sugars are left behind. It's these unfermentable complex sugars that will do much to determine how many carbohydrates will be left in the finished product—the more complex sugars left behind, the more resultant carbohydrates—all of this dependent on the style of beer desired and the type of yeast that is used for fermentation.

For those of you who still hold on to the incorrect notion that the sugars left behind in beer, especially maltose, are significant–they typically aren't. Go to *www.drinkbeer-getthindiet.com/f_a_q_s.htm* to see an analysis of various beer styles with their residual sugar contents.

Label Differences Between Light and Regular-Brewed Beers

Some breweries were amazingly cooperative in providing carbohydrate information for all their products, including Anheuser-Busch, Miller, Coors, and Pabst. But for every single brewery that offered nutritional analysis information of their products, there were ten others that did not. The Bureau of Alcohol, Tobacco and Firearms (now TTB) regulations did not require a nutritional analysis (calorie, carbohydrate, protein, and fat content) of beer produced or imported into the United States on containerized products (bottles, cans, etc.) unless the beers were indicated as being "light" or "lite." The ATF's explanation was as follows:

> *On August 10, 1993, the Bureau of Alcohol, Tobacco and Firearms (ATF) published an advanced notice of proposed rulemaking (ANPRM) in the Federal Register soliciting comments from the public and industry on whether the regulations should be amended to require nutritional information on labels of alcohol beverages.*
>
> *The comment period for the ANPRM closed on February 7, 1994.*

ATF received 55 comments in response to the advance notice. Only 7 of these comments came from consumers. However, 5 of the 7 consumers who commented opposed nutrition labeling. Overall, 80 percent of the comments received in response to the ANPRM opposed nutrition labeling for alcohol beverages. Thirty-five of the comments opposing nutrition labeling were submitted on behalf of industry, both domestic and foreign.

After careful consideration of the petition and the comments received in response to the advance notice, ATF determined that an amendment of the regulations to provide nutrition information on labels of alcohol beverages is unnecessary and unwarranted.

Could a brewery voluntarily add carbohydrate or caloric information to all their containerized products if they wanted to? For years, the answer was an emphatic "No." The old Bureau of Alcohol, Tobacco and Firearms proved to be adamant in their stern advice that " . . . nutrition information on labels [and cans] is unnecessary and unwarranted."

In the early 1990s, apparently to prove a point, the ATF brought the owner of a brewpub to court when he began to put nutritional information on the label of one of his regular-brewed beers—something his customers had asked for. A compromise was eventually reached between the ATF and the Yakima Brewing Company that allowed brewer Bert Grant to place the carbohydrate and fat content on the labels of his Scottish Ale. After watching the trouble and legal expenses that Grant had to contend with, the U.S. brewing industry refused to follow Grant's lead.

The revised statutes on nutritional information on beers also left the consumer without a way of backing out the reduced calorie or carbohydrate information that was often used as a point of comparison between a brewery's light and regular-brewed products. Up until 1994, a label on a light beer or in related advertising materials often boasted that the light beer product had "half the carbohydrates" or "one-third less calories" than its regular-brewed big brother, and then listed the carbs and calories. At the time, it was easy for beer drinkers to do the math and figure out how many calories or carbohydrates were in the same brand of regular-brewed beer by backing out the numbers. That numeric exercise, however, is no longer an option. According to the revised ATF Ruling 76-1, ATF C.B. 1976, 82:

> *In reviewing its position, the Bureau has found that specifying the caloric content of the product in comparison to the brewer's regular product is no longer essential to give the consumer a point of reference. Also, the Bureau has determined that carbohydrate references should be handled in the same manner as caloric references.*

Since light beers are lower in carbohydrates and calories than regular-brewed products, brewers have been forced to add this information in the form of an average nutritional analysis data sheet to their bottles, cans, and advertising in order to conform to ATF regulations—and as a sublime sales inducement for those trying to restrict their carbohydrate or calorie intake. From the revised ATF Ruling 76-1, ATF C.B. 1976, 82:

> *The Bureau will not sanction any caloric or carbohydrate references on labels that do not contain a statement of average analysis.*

The more savvy brewers, however, have made complete nutritional analyses of all their products and offer this information through handouts and product specification sheets to anyone who wants to know the nutritional values in what they're drinking.

As mentioned earlier, the ATF has recently been replaced by the Alcohol and Tobacco Tax and Trade Bureau. The TTB is seemingly a bit more enlightened as to the demands of today's consumers (including low-carb dieters) and now allows voluntary "directional health labeling" on alcoholic beverages, though consumers have thus far seen little movement by the manufacturers of alcoholic drinks to comply. Directional labels would not constitute a health claim, per se, but would instead guide consumers to government-sanctioned, health-related information or advice from medical experts about the possible benefits of moderate drinking. It's not complete nutritional labeling, but the door has now been opened for those drink manufacturers who also want to voluntarily add calorie and carbohydrate information on the labels of their products.

Just how accurate must the labeled carbohydrate counts for beer be? From the ATF/TTB:

> *The statements of carbohydrate and fat contents on labels for malt beverages will be considered acceptable as long as the carbohydrate and fat contents, as determined by ATF analysis, are within a reasonable range below the labeled amount but, in no case, are more than 20% above the labeled amount. For example, a label showing 4.0 grams (within good manufacturing practice limitations) but not more than 4.8 grams.*

A similar guideline holds for calories:

> *The statement of caloric content on labels for malt beverages will be considered acceptable as long as the caloric content, as determined by ATF analysis, is within the tolerance +5 and -10 calories of the labeled caloric content. For example a label showing 96 calories will be acceptable if ATF analysis of the product shows a caloric content between 86 and 101 calories.*

How popular are low-carb/-calorie beers, the only beers that display nutritional analyses? Bud Light is now the number-one selling beer in the United States. Notice it is the "number-one selling beer," not just the top-selling light beer. Anheuser-Busch's Michelob Ultra spilled well over the 2 million-barrel sale mark in its first year of production, making it one of the St. Louis-based brewery's most successful beer-product launches ever. Ultra has been particularly successful because of its labeling and marketing approach as a "low-carb" beer, a term that has recently been defined by the TTB as any beer with a carbohydrate count of 7 grams or less per serving.

What's amazing, however, is the reaction by competitors to Michelob Ultra. Miller Lite, now owned by South African Breweries (SAB), has decided to peck away at Bud Light, Amstel, and other brands that have higher carbohydrate counts than Miller Lite at 3.2 carbs per 12-ounce serving. To watch a Lite commercial, you'd never know that Michelob Ultra was even on the market. It's sound strategy by Miller—don't pick a fight you can't win! Brewing industry insiders think that the Miller Brewing Company is readying an even lower-carb beer than Lite that will eventually take on Michelob Ultra head to head, and probably be tagged as "low-carb," too. In the meantime, a whole slew of low-carb beers keep pouring into the market, including Latrobe's Rock Green Light and Sleeman's Clear out of Canada, and Aspen Edge, the latest low-carb beer entry by the Coors Brewing Company.

All of this makes me wonder. At what point, if ever, will beer drinkers possibly decide that taste wins over lower and lower-carb beers? Who knows? Thirty years ago, nobody had ever heard of light beers. For years they were disdained by beer drinkers, especially men. This beer category now holds close to 50 percent of the market. This isn't to say that low-carb or light beers don't have their own merits, especially in the early stages of any LC diet when carb intake is restricted or when someone simply counting carbs is near the end of his allowable carbohydrate intake for the day. One or two low-carb or light beers might be just the thing rather than a regular beer. As I've noted before, it's all in the numbers—and what you do with them.

If you can't find your favorite brew among those listed in the next chapter and would like to include it in your diet, I would suggest you call or write the brewery and ask if they can provide you with relevant carbohydrate information or simply switch to one of the fine brands listed here.

Many of the beer carbohydrate counts in the next chapter have been provided by cooperative breweries and brewpubs throughout the United States, Canada, Australia, New Zealand, Europe, and Asia, and in correspondences with brewery personnel. Some carbohydrate numbers for beers also came from the Siebel Institute of Technology. They published a number of beer carb counts from 1994–1999 in a trade report called *Beer Market*. A minority of the beer carbs (<10% or so) were derived from standard formulas using the stated alcohol by volume (ABV) and alcohol by weight (ABW), and the original gravities (OG) and final gravities (FG) of the product—the measure of the sugar content in beer before and after fermentation. This information was found on the Web sites of breweries (mostly the smaller ones) and more often through the brewers themselves.

These figures should be used as flexible guidelines only. Larger breweries can and do reformulate their brews on occasion, but usually not in significant measures. Smaller-sized regional breweries, microbreweries, and brewpubs, however, are a different story. There is sometimes more of an "art" involved in their brewing procedures that can lead to inconsistencies in successive batches of beer; this is a fact that some brewers will readily admit to and one that leads to the understanding of what the term "craft brewery" really means. Smaller breweries may also experiment with product lines and tweak their product formulations or change supply vendors—all variables that can change carbohydrate counts in their beers.

Also keep in mind that breweries do go out of business—an unfortunate occurrence for the brewery owners and their customers. By the time this book gets to store shelves, some breweries and their brands listed will have disappeared and others brought online. There might also be very old or very recent beer carbohydrate numbers that are in the public domain that are slightly different from those listed below.

Some breweries only bottle their beers in 750 ml containers versus the typical American 12-ounce (355 ml) bottles and cans. The carbohydrate listing for these larger bottles have been figured at the smaller 12-ounce-size serving size unless noted otherwise.

Please also note that the states of Utah, Colorado, Kansas, Oklahoma, and certain counties restrict the alcoholic content of beer sold in their areas. These beers are referred to in the following list as 3.2 [%]. Coors also uses the term "Repeal" to indicate a full strength beer.

For more information and an expanded list of updates and corrections to the carbohydrate counts of beers as they become available, check our Web sites at *www.DrinkBeer-GetThinDiet.com* and *www.LCBartender.com*.

The following information is provided as a general guide of beer and carbohydrate levels for those wishing to follow a low-carbohydrate approach to dieting. It is not a substitute for specific advice from your general practitioner.

3

Carbohydrate Counts of Beer

REMEMBER—the TTB allows a reasonable carbohydrate range below the carb count of the beer, but in no case does it allow more than 20% above the carb count. Since there's no indication of what the TTB actually interprets as a "reasonable" amount (5-10-20%), but gives a leeway of up to 20% above the listed amount—I'm assuming that a beer with a content of 20 carbohydrates, for instance, might actually range anywhere between 20% below or 20% above the stated value, i.e., 16 to 24 carbs per serving in the case of a stated carbohydrate content of 20 grams per serving.

Abita		
Turbodog	12 oz	19.25 g
Purple Haze	12 oz	14.25 g
American Wheat	12 oz	13.65 g
Stout	12 oz	19.75 g

Alaskan

Amber (Alt)	12 oz	17 g
ESB	12 oz	17 g
Pale	12 oz	13 g
Smoked Porter	12 oz	37 g
Summer Kolsch	12 oz	12 g
Oatmeal Stout	12 oz	24 g
Winter Old Ale	12 oz	22 g

Alley Kat

Amber	12 oz	16 g
Aprikat	12 oz	12.1 g
Full Moon	12 oz	14.75 g

Alpine

Ale	12 oz	11.25 g
Captain Stout	12 oz	17 g
Mandarin Nectar	12 oz	9.25 g
Mcllenney's Irish Red	12 oz	13.25 g
Pure Hoppiness	12 oz	16.25 g
Willy	12 oz	7.5 g
Willy Vanilly	12 oz	7.5 g

Alpirsbacher Klosterbrauerei

Spezial	12 oz	15.95 g
Pils	12 oz	15.45 g
Kloster Dunkel	12 oz	15.95 g
Light	12 oz	9.6 g
Kloster Weisse Dunkel	12 oz	13.2 g
Kloster Wesse Hefetrub	12 oz	18.65 g
Kloster Krystalklar	12 oz	13.2 g

Amstel

Amstel	12 oz	10.65 g
Bock	12 oz	17.75 g
Gold	12 oz	14.2 g
Lentebock	12 oz	17.74 g
Light	12 oz	5.33 g
Meibock	12 oz	17.75 g
Malt	12 oz	21.3 g
Oud Bruin	12 oz	19.52 g
1870	12 oz	12.42 g

Anchor

Anchor Porter	12 oz	23.53 g
Anchor Steam	12 oz	15 g

Anderson Valley

Barney Flats Oatmeal Stout	12 oz	22.1 g
Belk's ESB	12 oz	18.5 g
Boont Amber Ale	12 oz	15.8 g
Deependers Dark Porter	12 oz	15.3 g
High Rollers Wheat Ale	12 oz	13.4 g
Hop Ottin' IPA	12 oz	18.8 g
Poleeko Gold Pale Ale	12 oz	14.4 g
Winter Solstice Seasonal Ale	12 oz	17.6 g

Anheuser-Busch

180 High Energy Drink	8.2 oz	33 g
Bacardi Silver	12 oz	34.7 g
Bacardi Silver O3	12 oz	32.7 g
Budweiser	12 oz	10.6 g
Budweiser 3.2	12 oz	8.7 g
Bud Light	12 oz	6.6 g

Anheuser-Busch (continued)

Bud Light 3.2	12 oz	5.2 g
Bud Ice	12 oz	9 g
Bud Ice Light	12 oz	5.2 g
Bud Ice Light 3.2	12 oz	3.6 g
Bud Dry	12 oz	7.8 g
Bud Dry 3.2	12 oz	6.3 g
Doc's Hard Lemon	12 oz	16.5 g
Maerzen	12 oz	15 g
Michelob	12 oz	13 g
Michelob 3.2	12 oz	12.2 g
Michelob Light	12 oz	11.7 g
Michelob Light 3.2	12 oz	9.3 g
Michelob Ultra	12 oz	2.6 g
Michelob Golden Draft	12 oz	12.9 g
Michelob Golden Draft 3.2	12 oz	10.5 g
Michelob Golden Draft Light	12 oz	7 g
Michelob Golden Draft Light 3.2	12 oz	5.5 g
Michelob Dry	12 oz	7.9 g
Michelob Classic Dark	12 oz	14.5 g
Michelob Amber Bock	12 oz	14.5 g
Michelob Amber Bock 3.2	12 oz	11.9 g
Michelob Hefeweizen	12 oz	16.9 g
Michelob Hefeweizen 3.2	12 oz	11.9 g
Michelob Porter	12 oz	20.2 g
Michelob Pale Ale	12 oz	16.7 g
Michelob Honey Lager	12 oz	17.9 g
Michelob Honey Lager 3.2	12 oz	14.9 g
Michelob Black & Tan	12 oz	16.3 g
Red Wolf	12 oz	11.7 g
Red Wolf 3.2	12 oz	9.2 g

O'Doul's	12 oz	13.3 g
O'Doul's Amber	12 oz	18 g
Busch	12 oz	10 g
Busch 3.2	12 oz	8.1 g
Busch NA	12 oz	12.9 g
Busch Light	12 oz	6.7 g
Busch Light 3.2	12 oz	5.2 g
Busch Ice	12 oz	13.2 g
Busch Ice 3.2	12 oz	10.3 g
Natural Light	12 oz	6.6 g
Natural Light 3.2	12 oz	5.3 g
Natural Ice	12 oz	9.4 g
Natural Ice 3.2	12 oz	7.6 g
King Cobra	12 oz	15.4 g
Hurricane	12 oz	9.6 g
Tequiza	12 oz	9.1 g
Tequiza 3.2	12 oz	9 g
ZeigenBock	12 oz	14.4 g

Appalachian

Winter Gap Wheat	12 oz	14.4 g
Mountain Lager	12 oz	18 g
Purist Pale Ale	12 oz	16.7 g
Jolly Scot Ale	12 oz	19.35 g
Susquehanna Stout	12 oz	22.35 g

Arbor

Bavarian Bliss Hefeweizen	12 oz	16.4 g
Big Ben House Mild	12 oz	14.8 g
Faricy Fest Irish Stout	12 oz	16.8 g
Huxell Best Bitter	12 oz	15.5 g
Jackhammer Old Ale	12 oz	27.4 g

Arbor (continued)

Milestone Porter	12 oz	20.7 g
Olde Number 22 German Alt	12 oz	17 g
Red Snapper Special Bitter	12 oz	16.4 g
Sacred Cow IPA	12 oz	18.2 g
Terminator Dopplebock	12 oz	31 g

Ashai

Dry	12 oz	10.43 g

Ashauer

Dunkel	12 oz	15.25 g
Hell	12 oz	14.75 g
Prima Weisse Dunkel	12 oz	15.25 g

Atlanta

Brick House Premium Lager	12 oz	9.7 g
Kelly's Light	12 oz	4.6 g
Laughing Skull Pilsner	12 oz	9.7 g
Peachtree Pale Ale	12 oz	9.9 g
Red Brick Ale	12 oz	10.5 g

August Schell

Blizzard Ale	12 oz	13.65 g
Light	12 oz	4 g

Baltika, Russia

Baltika N1 Light	12 oz	15.77 g
Baltika N0 Non-alcoholic	12 oz	15.77 g
Baltika N3 Classic	12 oz	16.46 g
Baltika N4 Original	12 oz	16.46 g
Baltika N6 Porter	12 oz	20.57 g

Baltika N7 Export	12 oz	15.43 g
Baltika N8 Wheat	12 oz	11.66 g
Baltika N9 Strong	12 oz	12.64 g
Baltika Jubilee Beer	12 oz	14.4 g
Parnassus	12 oz	16.56 g
Medovoye (Honey) Light	12 oz	15.77 g
Medovoye (Honey) Extra	12 oz	22.63 g
Don 1	12 oz	15.77 g
Don 5	12 oz	22.63 g

Baltimore-Washington Beer Works

Raven Special	12 oz	18.5 g

Bass

Pale Ale	12 oz	12.5 g

Beck's

Beck's	12 oz	10 g
Beck's Dark	12 oz	11 g
Beck's Light	12 oz	6.1 g
Beck's Oktoberfest	12 oz	9 g
Clausthaler Golden	12 oz	15.98 g
Clausthaler Premium	12 oz	19.32 g
Dribeck	12 oz	7 g
Hacke Beck NA	12 oz	20 g
St. Pauli Girl	12 oz	8.7 g
St. Pauli Girl NA	12 oz	23 g

Big Rock

All Brands	12 oz	12.7 g
Jack Rabbit	12 oz	2 g

Big Time

Nemesis Strong Ale	12 oz	26.5 g

Bison

Organic Light	12 oz	8.8 g

Bitburger

Pils	12 oz	9.05 g
Light	12 oz	7.1 g
Drive NA	12 oz	20.59 g
Koestritzer	12 oz	9.94 g
Kandi	12 oz	35.5 g

Blitz-Weinhard

Private Reserve	12 oz	13.8 g
Weinhard's Ale	12 oz	13.5 g
H.W.'s Amber Ale	12 oz	16.85 g
H.W.'s Porter	12 oz	23.8 g
H.W.'s Blackberry Wheat	12 oz	13.35 g

Bochkarev

Export	12 oz	13.49 g
Light	12 oz	13.49 g
Strong	12 oz	21.3 g
Barreled	12 oz	9.94 g
Wheat Special	12 oz	15.98 g
Non-Alcoholic	12 oz	21.66 g

Boddingtons

Boddingtons Pub Ale	12 oz	12.78 g

Boston Beer Company

Boston Ale	12 oz	19.9 g
Boston Lager	12 oz	18 g
Cherry Wheat	12 oz	16.86 g
Cranberry Lambic	12 oz	20.91 g
Cream Stout	12 oz	23.94 g
Double Bock	12 oz	32.4 g
Golden Pilsner	12 oz	15.75 g
Hardcore Crisp Cider	12 oz	19 g
Honey Porter	12 oz	20.57 g
Light	12 oz	9.7 g
Octoberfest	12 oz	18.72 g
Scotch Ale	12 oz	24.96 g
Spring Ale (Kolsch)	12 oz	16.53 g
Summer Ale	12 oz	15.85 g
White Ale	12 oz	16.86 g
Winter Lager	12 oz	21.25 g

Boulevard

Unfiltered Wheat	12 oz	12.6 g

Brand

Dubbelbock	12 oz	17.75 g
Imperator	12 oz	14.2 g
Meibock	12 oz	14.2 g
Oud Bruin	12 oz	7.1 g
Pilsner	12 oz	10.65 g
Sylvester	12 oz	17.75 g
UP	12 oz	12.43 g
Vos	12 oz	14.2 g
Wieckse Witte	12 oz	12.42 g

Bristol

Beehive Honey Wheat	12 oz	17 g
Laughing Lab Scottish Ale	12 oz	22 g
Mass Transit Ale	12 oz	18.2 g
Old No. 23 Barley Wine	12 oz	31.6 g
Red Rocket Pale Ale	12 oz	15.75 g

Brouwerij Martens

Martens Low Carbohydrate	275 ml	2.1 g

Buckhead

Black Diamond Stout	12 oz	16.5 g
Buck Light	12 oz	8.45 g
Panther Pale Ale	12 oz	19.9 g
Red Hills Ale	12 oz	16.7 g

Budweiser Budvar (also known as Checkvar)

Budvar Free (NA)	12 oz	9.23 g
Budejovicky Budvar (10%)	12 oz	13.49 g
Budejovicky Budvar (12%)	12 oz	14.42 g
Bud Super Strong (16%)	12 oz	16.45 g

Caledonian

125	12 oz	12.6 g
Burke & Hare	12 oz	13.49 g
Burns Ale	12 oz	14.35 g
Calders 70/-	12 oz	9.45 g
Calders 80/-	12 oz	10.5 g
Calders Cream	12 oz	12.07 g
Calders Light	12 oz	11.72 g
Caley 80/-	12 oz	13.16 g
Golden Promise	12 oz	13.85 g

Grand Slam	12 oz	12.78 g
IPA	12 oz	12.43 g
Summer Ale	12 oz	9.59 g
Festival	12 oz	12.07 g
Mellow Yellow	12 oz	12.43 g
Space Odessy	12 oz	10.3 g

Cambridge

Benevolence	12 oz	24.25 g
Cambridge Amber	12 oz	16.4 g
Charles River Porter	12 oz	19.8 g
Off- (Trap)Piste Belgian-Style Grand Cru	12 oz	23.5 g
Regatta Golden	12 oz	13.9 g
Tall Tale Pale Ale	12 oz	18.7 g
Triple Threat	12 oz	22.7 g
Winter Ale	12 oz	20.35 g

Carlsberg

Light	12 oz	7.81 g
Lager	12 oz	9.94 g
Red	12 oz	10.3 g
Red Elephant	12 oz	11.72 g
Elephant Malt Liquor	12 oz	14.2 g

Carolina Beer & Beverage Company

Carolina Light	12 oz	2 g
Charleston Wheat	12 oz	5 g

Cascade Lakes

20" Brown	12 oz	17.15 g
Blonde Bombshell	12 oz	12 g
Fat Fish Pale Ale	12 oz	14.7 g

Cascade Lakes (continued)

Grizzly Mountain Stout	12 oz	21.4 g
IPA	12 oz	17.4 g
MacDougal's Amber	12 oz	16.55 g
Monkey Face Porter	12 oz	18.5 g
Rooster Tail Ale	12 oz	15.15 g
Santa's Little Helper	12 oz	21.5 g
Weiss	12 oz	15.15 g

Cedar

Black Cobra Stout	12 oz	10.6 g
Dunkel Weisse	12 oz	10.3 g
Flying Aces Ale	12 oz	10.8 g
Golden Hawk	12 oz	10 g
Helles Honey Bock	12 oz	11.5 g
Oatmeal Stout	12 oz	11.8 g
Oktoberfest	12 oz	10 g
Red Rocket Amber Ale	12 oz	10.3 g
Sassy Lassy	12 oz	10 g
Victory Cream Ale	12 oz	8.7 g

Celis

White	12 oz	13.9 g
Pale Bock	12 oz	13.3 g
Raspberry	12 oz	13.9 g
Grand Cru	12 oz	16 g
Golden	12 oz	15.1 g
Dubbel Ale	12 oz	16.4 g

Cisco

Whale's Tale Pale Ale	12 oz	13.5 g

Clausthaler

Premium Non-Alcoholic	12 oz	20.6 g

Coast Range

California Blonde	12 oz	16.25 g
Pale Ale	12 oz	20 g

Coastal Extreme

Newport Storm Hurricane Amber	12 oz	12 g

Companhia Cervejaria

Brahma	12 oz	13.63 g

Cooper's

Genuine Draught	12 oz	7.02 g
Lite	12 oz	4.5 g
Sparkling Ale	12 oz	7.56 g
Stout	12 oz	10.8 g
Pale Ale	12 oz	5.94 g
Premium	12 oz	11.52 g
Export	12 oz	11.16 g
Dry	12 oz	6.84 g

Cooperstown

Old Slugger	12 oz	17.3 g
Benchwarmer	12 oz	19.3 g
Nine Man Ale	12 oz	15.15 g
Strike Out Stout	12 oz	17.75 g

Coors

Aspen Edge	12 oz	2.5 g
Artic Ice Repeal	12 oz	8.98 g
Artic Ice 3.2	12 oz	6.66 g
Artic Ice Export	12 oz	5.82 g
Blue Moon Belgian White	12 oz	12.87 g
Blue Moon Honey Blond Repeal	12 oz	19.72 g
Blue Moon Nut Brown Repeal	12 oz	16.78 g
Blue Moon Raspberry Repeal	12 oz	20.92 g
Castlemaine XXXX Repeal	12 oz	9.41 g
Coors Repeal	12 oz	11.79 g
Coors 3.2	12 oz	9.54 g
Coors Export	12 oz	10.68 g
Coors Light Repeal	12 oz	4.32 g
Coors Light 3.2	12 oz	4.12 g
Coors Light Export	12 oz	3.98 g
Coors Dry Repeal	12 oz	5.92 g
Coors Dry	12 oz	4.84 g
Cutter	12 oz	15.65 g
Cutter Export	12 oz	15.28 g
Extra Gold Repeal	12 oz	11.65 g
Extra Gold 3.2	12 oz	9.35 g
Extra Gold Export	12 oz	10.58 g
Herman Joseph Repeal	12 oz	12.21 g
Killian's	12 oz	15 g
Killian's 3.2%	12 oz	11 g
Winterfest (seasonal)	12 oz	16–18 g
Zima Gold	12 oz	9.73 g

Crooked River

Crooked River Expansion Draft	12 oz	13 g
Crooked River Select Lager	12 oz	15.7 g

DB Breweries

DB Draught	12 oz	9.6 g
DB Natural	12 oz	9.6 g
DB Natural Light	12 oz	9.6 g
DB Bitter	12 oz	9.6 g
Double Brown	12 oz	9.6 g
Export Gold	12 oz	9.6 g
Tui EIPA	12 oz	9.6 g
Export Dry	12 oz	10.29 g
Flame	12 oz	10.29 g
Monteith's Pilsener	12 oz	10.29 g
Monteith's Golden	12 oz	10.29 g
Monteith's Celtic Red	12 oz	12 g
Monteith's Black	12 oz	15.43 g
Monteith's Original	12 oz	15.43 g
Vita Stout	12 oz	15.43 g

Deschutes

Bachelor ESB	12 oz	18.8 g
Black Butte	12 oz	18.85 g
Cascade	12 oz	14.25 g
Mirror Pond Pale Ale	12 oz	17.4 g
Obsidian	12 oz	20.5 g
Quail Springs IPA	12 oz	19.4 g

Diamond Knot

Golden Ale	12 oz	14.85 g
Hefe-Weizen	12 oz	17.9 g
Icebreaker Barley Wine	12 oz	25 g
Industrial Ho!Ho!	12 oz	22.8 g
Industrial IPA	12 oz	21.3 g

Diamond Knot (continued)

IPA	12 oz	17.25 g
Possession Porter	12 oz	17 g
Rivertown Brown Ale	12 oz	17 g
Steamer Glide Stout	12 oz	15 g

Dortmunder Aktien (DAB)

Diät Pils	500 ml (½ liter)	3.5 g

Fearless

American Brown	12 oz	20 g
Hefeweizen	12 oz	22 g
Pale Ale	12 oz	23.5 g
Porter	12 oz	22 g
Scottish Ale	12 oz	24 g

FEMSA

Dos Equis Amber Lager	12 oz	12.87 g
Tecate	12 oz	12.5 g

Firestone Walker

Coastal Light	12 oz	3.9 g
Coastal Light Pale Ale	12 oz	5.4 g

Fitger's

El Nino Double-Hopped IPA	12 oz	20 g
Lighthouse Golden	12 oz	11 g
Mariner Mild	12 oz	13.75 g
Park Point Pilsener	12 oz	11 g

Flat Branch

Brown	12 oz	23.7 g
Green Chili	12 oz	17.45 g
Honey Wheat	12 oz	19.75 g
Hudson ESB	12 oz	25 g
IPA	12 oz	22.75 g
Katy Trail Pale Ale	12 oz	18.6 g
Lager	12 oz	19.05 g
Oil Change Stout	12 oz	22.8 g

Flying Fish

Porter	12 oz	19 g
Belgian Ale Double	12 oz	15.75 g
ESB	12 oz	19.9 g
Extra Pale Ale	12 oz	14.4 g

Foster's

Abbotsford Invalid Stout	12 oz	11.76 g
Cairns Draught	12 oz	9.94 g
Carlton Black Ale	12 oz	10.65 g
Carlton Cold Filtered Bitter	12 oz	9.94 g
Carlton Draught	12 oz	9.59 g
Carlton G	12 oz	9.59 g
Carlton Light	12 oz	10.65 g
Carlton Light NT	12 oz	9.59 g
Carlton LJ	12 oz	3.2 g
Carlton Mid Strength Bitter	12 oz	14.2 g
Carlton Mid Strength Bitter QLD	12 oz	14.56 g
Carlton Premium Dry	12 oz	9.94 g
Cascade Bitter	12 oz	9.59 g
Cascade Draught	12 oz	9.23 g
Cascade Lager	12 oz	9.59 g

Foster's (continued)

Cascade Pale Ale	12 oz	9.94 g
Cascade Premium	12 oz	11 g
Cascade Premium Light	12 oz	11.36 g
Cascade Stout	12 oz	15.98 g
Crown Lager	12 oz	11 g
Dogbolter	12 oz	14.2 g
Fiji Bitter	12 oz	9.94 g
Fiji Gold	12 oz	5.68 g
Foster's Ice	12 oz	11.36 g
Foster's Lager	12 oz	11 g
Foster's Light-NZ	12 oz	10.3 g
Foster's Light Ice	12 oz	11 g
Foster's Special Bitter	12 oz	12.78 g
Guinness Draught	12 oz	12.78 g
Guinness	12 oz	17.4 g
303 Ice Gold	12 oz	11.76 g
KB Lager	12 oz	11 g
Kent Old Brown	12 oz	11.36 g
Matilda Bay Bitter	12 oz	15.27 g
Matilda Bay Premium	12 oz	12.78 g
Melbourne Bitter	12 oz	11 g
NT Draught	12 oz	9.94 g
Power's Bitter	12 oz	9.94 g
Power's Gold	12 oz	9.23 g
Power's Ice	12 oz	8.88 g
Redback Light	12 oz	9.59 g
Redback Original	12 oz	12.78 g
Resch's DA	12 oz	11.76 g
Resch's Draught	12 oz	9.94 g
Resch's Pilsener	12 oz	10.3 g
Resch's Pilsener (New Zealand)	12 oz	8.88 g

Resch's Real Bitter	12 oz	10.65 g
Resch's Real Bitter (New Zealand)	12 oz	10.65 g
Richmond Lager	12 oz	9.94 g
Sheaf Stout	12 oz	18.82 g
Stella Artois	12 oz	12.78 g
Victoria Bitter	12 oz	11 g
Yatala Stripe	12 oz	12.78 g

Frederick

Blue Ridge Amber Ale	12 oz	19.25 g
BR Dopplebock	12 oz	26.9 g
BR ESB Red Ale	12 oz	16.4 g
BR Golden Ale	12 oz	17.15 g
BR Hopfest	12 oz	16.25 g
BR Porter	12 oz	23.25 g
BR Sour Mash Ale	12 oz	27.4 g
BR Steeple Stout	12 oz	28.3 g
BR Wheat Beer	12 oz	12.85 g
BR Winter Ale	12 oz	22.35 g
Crooked River Light	12 oz	6.4 g
Hempen Gold	12 oz	16.2 g
Hempen Ale	12 oz	22 g

Goose Island

American Wheat "312"	12 oz	10.5 g
Blonde Ale	12 oz	12 g
Christmas Ale	12 oz	25 g
Hex Nut Brown	12 oz	16.5 g
Honker's Ale	12 oz	16.5 g
India Pale Ale	12 oz	21.5 g
Kilgubbin Irish Red Ale	12 oz	15 g
Oatmeal Stout	12 oz	24 g

Goose Island (continued)

Oktoberfest Lager	12 oz	17 g
Pils Lager	12 oz	13 g
Summertime Kolsch	12 oz	13.5 g

Gorden Biersch

Blonde Bock	12 oz	15.81 g

Granite

Best Bitter	12 oz	17.5 g
Best Bitter Special	12 oz	16.1 g
IPA	12 oz	17 g
Keefe's Irish Stout	12 oz	17.9 g
Peculiar	12 oz	19.2 g
Ringberry	12 oz	17.5 g
Ringwood	12 oz	17.5 g
Summer Ale	12 oz	14.5 g

Grant's

Scottish Ale	12 oz	12.7 g

Great Beer

Hollywood Blonde Kolsch	12 oz	14.21 g

Great Divide

Arapahoe Amber	12 oz	18.85 g
Bee Sting	12 oz	14.85 g
Denver Pale Ale (DPA)	12 oz	16.2 g
Fresh Hop	12 oz	19 g
Hercules Double IPA	12 oz	29.5 g
Hibernation	12 oz	26.5 g
St. Brigid's Porter	12 oz	17.6 g

Titan IPA	12 oz	21 g
Wild Raspberry Ale	12 oz	15.45 g
Yeti Imperial Stout	12 oz	35.6 g

Grolsch

Amber	12 oz	11.36 g
Herfstbok	12 oz	15.62 g
Lentebok	12 oz	12.07 g
Oud Bruin	12 oz	12.78 g
Premium Pilsner	12 oz	11 g
Special Malt	12 oz	18.46 g
Wintarvorst	12 oz	17.4 g
Zomergoud	12 oz	11.36 g

Grupo Modelo

Corona Extra	12 oz	13.99 g
Corona Light	12 oz	5 g
Negra Modelo	12 oz	14 g

Guinness*

Guinness Draught	12 oz	10 g
Guinness Extra Stout	12 oz	14 g
Harp Lager	12 oz	13 g
Kaliber	12 oz	10.3 g

*Note about Guinness

Guinness is brewed in fifty-one countries and the carbohydrate count for this product varies from an anecdotal 5.20 grams of carbohydrates per 12-ounce serving (from *Stout* by Michael J. Lewis; Brewers Publications, 1995), up to a documented 17 grams or so, depending on where it's brewed. The home office for Guinness (Diageo) says a 12-ounce serving comes in at 10 carbs. The Guinness in Australia, however, hits the high end, though with no understanding as to why. A recent check was just done with the Lion-Nathan Brewery for their version of Guinness Draught for New Zealand—5.50 carbs in a 12-ounce serving. In Nigeria, Africa, where three Guinness breweries are located, local grains such as maize and sorghum are used in the dark brew. Analyses of Guinness Stout done in 1995 and 1998 at the lab services division of the Siebel Institute of Technology, puts the carb count for a 12-ounce serving at 13.79 and 9.98 respectively.

So how many carbs in Guinness? Which Guinness and from where? I give up!

My suggestion? When in doubt, remember that the draught (draft) version hits the lower end of the carb range.

Harpoon

IPA	12 oz	14.5–16.5 g

Heavenly Daze

Power Daze Ale	12 oz	10 g

Heineken

Eindejaars Bier	12 oz	19.53 g
Heineken	12 oz	10.65 g
Heineken Oud Bruin	12 oz	19.7 g
Heineken Tarwebok	12 oz	23.08 g
Kylian	12 oz	23.08 g
Lingen's Blond	12 oz	17.75 g
Vollenhoven's Stout	12 oz	19.53 g

High Falls

Dundee's Classic Lager	12 oz	13 g
Genesee Beer	12 oz	13.5 g
Genesee Cream Ale	12 oz	15 g
Genesee Ice	12 oz	12 g
Genny Light	12 oz	5.5 g
Genesee NA	12 oz	15 g
Genesee Red	12 oz	14 g
Kipling Light Lager	12 oz	8 g
12 Horse	12 oz	14 g
Honey Brown Lager	12 oz	13.5 g
Honey Brown Light	12 oz	7.7 g
Honey Brown Light >3.2	12 oz	9.3 g
Michael Shea's Irish Amber	12 oz	13 g
Michael Shea's Black & Tan	12 oz	13 g

Holsten

Duckstein	12 oz	10.65 g
Export	12 oz	8.88 g
Franziskaner	12 oz	10.3 g
König Pilsener	12 oz	9.59 g
Non-Alcoholic	12 oz	17.75 g
Pils	12 oz	7.1 g

Hops Grillhouse & Brewery

Alligator Ale	12 oz	14.75 g
Clearwater Light	12 oz	9.34 g
Hammerhead Red	12 oz	12.6 g
Lightening Bold Gold	12 oz	11.84 g

Hudepohl-Schoenling

Burger Classic Beer	12 oz	12.4 g
Burger Light	12 oz	9.6 g
Christian Moerlein Select Lager	12 oz	15.7 g
Christian Moerlein Bock	12 oz	15.7 g
Hudy Delight Premium Light Beer	12 oz	3.7 g
Little Kings Cream Ale	12 oz	15.8 g
Hudepohl 14-K	12 oz	12.4 g
Schoenling Lager	12 oz	12.4 g

Independence

IPA	12 oz	17.8 g
Kolsch	12 oz	11.2 g
OMA	12 oz	23 g
Red Ale	12 oz	16.9 g

Kalamazoo

Bell's Amber Ale	12 oz	16.85 g
Bell's Cherry Stout	12 oz	26.1 g
Bell's Consecrator Doppelbock	12 oz	28.25 g
Bell's Expedition Stout	12 oz	34.7 g
Bell's Java Stout	12 oz	25 g
Bell's Kalamazoo Stout	12 oz	20.22 g
Bell's Oberon Ale	12 oz	17.75 g
Bell's Porter	12 oz	15.9 g
Bell's Sparkling Ale	12 oz	21.25 g

Bell's Special Double Cream Stout	12 oz	25 g
Bell's Winter White Ale	12 oz	15.5 g
Third Coast	12 oz	14.1 g
Two Hearted Ale	12 oz	18.7 g

Karlsburg

Rheinbecker Extra Bräu	12 oz	2.5 g

Kennebunkport/Shipyard

Old Thumper	12 oz	16.11 g

Kirin

Lager	12 oz	11.23 g

Kona

Fire Rock Pale Ale	12 oz	13.59 g
Longboard Lager	12 oz	13.28 g
Pacific Golden Ale	12 oz	11.51 g

Labatt

Blue	12 oz	10.51 g
Light	12 oz	7.9 g
Regular	12 oz	9.9 g
Sterling	12 oz	2.5 g

Latrobe

Rolling Green Light	12 oz	2.6 g
Rolling Rock	12 oz	10 g

Legend

Brown Ale	12 oz	19.8 g
Dopplebock	12 oz	25.4 g
Golden IPA	12 oz	21 g
Lager	12 oz	15.25 g
Oktoberfest	12 oz	19.25 g
Pilsner	12 oz	21.4 g
Porter	12 oz	24.2 g
Stout	12 oz	16.7 g

Leinenkugel

Amber Light	12 oz	7.4 g
Berry Weiss	12 oz	28 g
Big Butt	12 oz	18.8 g
Creamy Dark	12 oz	16.8 g
Honey Weiss	12 oz	12 g
Light	12 oz	5.7 g
Northwoods Lager	12 oz	15.3 g
Oktoberfest	12 oz	17.8 g
Original	12 oz	13.9 g
Red Lager	12 oz	16.2 g

Lion-Nathan

1857 Bitter	12 oz	10.85 g
Australian White Beer	12 oz	15.98 g
Canterbury Draught	12 oz	8.05 g
Carbine Stout	12 oz	14.35 g
Eagle Blue	12 oz	9.8 g
Eagle Blue Ice	12 oz	9.45 g
Eagle Super	12 oz	9.45 g
Emu Bitter	12 oz	12.78 g

Emu Draft	12 oz	10.85 g
Emu Export	12 oz	10.3 g
Emundi	12 oz	11 g
Guinness Draught (NZ)	12 oz	5.5 g
Gulf Lager	12 oz	10.85 g
Hahn Ice	12 oz	8.75 g
Hahn Longbrew	12 oz	4.55 g
Hahn Premium	12 oz	11.2 g
Hahn Premium Light	12 oz	10.85 g
Hahn Witbier	12 oz	9.94 g
Ice Beer	12 oz	8.05 g
James Squire Amber Ale	12 oz	14.91 g
James Squire Pilsener	12 oz	15.98 g
James Squire Porter	12 oz	14.91 g
Light Ice	12 oz	6.75 g
Lion Brown	12 oz	8.05 g
Lion Light Ice	12 oz	6.65 g
Lion Red	12 oz	7.7 g
Old Black Ale	12 oz	16.1 g
Rheineck	12 oz	12 g
Southwark Bitter	12 oz	9.94 g
Southwark Black Ale	12 oz	16.1 g
Southwark Pale Ale	12 oz	9.8 g
Southwark Premium	12 oz	10.15 g
Southwark Old Stout	12 oz	12.6 g
Southwark White	12 oz	10.3 g
Sovereign	12 oz	12.07 g
Speight's	12 oz	7.35 g
Speight's Old Ale	12 oz	10.15 g
Speights Old Dark	12 oz	10.3 g
Steinlager	12 oz	8.4 g
Steinlager (China)	12 oz	11.72 g

Lion-Nathan (continued)

Swan Draught	12 oz	10.15 g
Swan Gold	12 oz	9.1 g
Swan Mid	12 oz	13.65 g
Swan Stout	12 oz	12.6 g
Tooheys Amber Bitter	12 oz	10.85 g
Tooheys Blue	12 oz	15.75 g
Tooheys Blue Ice	12 oz	12.25 g
Tooheys Extra Dry	12 oz	8.75 g
Tooheys Gold	12 oz	10.85 g
Tooheys Maxim	12 oz	5.68 g
Tooheys New	12 oz	10.85 g
Tooheys Old	12 oz	11.2 g
Tooheys Pils	12 oz	8.91 g
Tooheys Red	12 oz	11.72 g
Waikato Draught	12 oz	7.1 g
West End 107 Pilsener	12 oz	9.94 g
West End Draught	12 oz	8.52 g
West End Export	12 oz	9.05 g
West End Gold	12 oz	8.17 g
West End Light	12 oz	7.46 g
XXXX Bitter	12 oz	8.17 g
XXXX DL Lager	12 oz	3.55 g
XXXX Draught	12 oz	8.17 g
XXXX Gold	12 oz	7.1 g

Long Beach

Thin Ice	12 oz	1 g

Lost Coast

Alleycat Amber	12 oz	13 g
Downtown Brown	12 oz	13 g
8-Ball Stout	12 oz	17 g
Great White	12 oz	13 g
Indica IPA	12 oz	13 g
Lost Coast Apricot Wheat	12 oz	9 g
Lost Coast Harvest Wheat	12 oz	9 g
Lost Coast Pale Ale	22 oz	22 g
Raspberry Brown	22 oz	22 g
Winterbraun	12 oz	9 g

Lovejoys

AJ Porter	12 oz	16.25 g
Atlas Stout	12 oz	15 g
Bolivar Blond Ale	12 oz	14.1 g
Hopper IPA	12 oz	19.15 g
Gala Oatmeal Stout	12 oz	15.25 g
Hollywood Hefeweizen	12 oz	12.25 g
Hop On Pop	12 oz	16.5 g
HyperAtlas Stout	12 oz	17.4 g
LOVE ESB	12 oz	17.2 g
October Ale	12 oz	17.25 g
Old 97 Steam Beer	12 oz	16 g
Old Whore	12 oz	18.75 g
Redd	12 oz	19.2 g
Sampson Pale Ale	12 oz	17.15 g
Sparky's Special Ale	12 oz	15.75 g

Mackeson

Stout	12 oz	16.33 g

Mad River

Jamaica Red	12 oz	20.25 g
Jamaica Sunset West Indies Pale Ale	12 oz	18.9 g
John Barleycorn Barleywine 2003	12 oz	35.5 g
Steelhead Extra Pale Ale	12 oz	16.7 g
Steelhead Extra Stout	12 oz	25.25 g
Steelhead Scotch Porter	12 oz	20.5 g

Matt

Accel	12 oz	2.4 g

McSorley's

Black & Tan	12 oz	19.4 g
Double Dark	12 oz	21 g
Ale	12 oz	16.5 g
Wintertime Ale	12 oz	18.8 g

Middle Ages

Grail Ale	12 oz	17.35 g
Beast Bitter	12 oz	17.75 g
White Knight Light Ale	12 oz	16.25 g

Mike's

Mike's Hard Cranberry Lemonade	12 oz	41 g
Mike's Hard Lemonade	12 oz	36 g

Miller

Miller Genuine Draft	12 oz	13.1 g
Genuine Draft Light	12 oz	7 g
Hamm's	12 oz	12.1 g
Hamm's Golden Draft	12 oz	12.1 g
Hamm's Special Light	12 oz	7.3 g

Henry Weinhard's Amber Ale	12 oz	14 g
Henry Weinhard's Dark	12 oz	13.1 g
Henry Weinhard's Hefeweizen	12 oz	12.1 g
Henry Weinhard's Ice Ale	12 oz	13.2 g
Henry Weinhard's Pale Ale	12 oz	13 g
Henry Weinhard's Private Reserve	12 oz	9.2 g
High Life	12 oz	13.1 g
High Life Ice	12 oz	11 g
High Life Light	12 oz	7 g
Icehouse 5.5	12 oz	9.8 g
Icehouse 5.0	12 oz	8.7 g
Lite Ice 5.5	12 oz	4.2 g
Magnum Malt Liquor	12 oz	9.9 g
Meister Brau	12 oz	11.4 g
Meister Brau Light	12 oz	4.8 g
Mickey's	12 oz	11.2 g
Mickey's Ice	12 oz	11.8 g
Miller Lite	12 oz	3.2 g
Milwaukee's Best	12 oz	11.4 g
Milwaukee's Best Ice	12 oz	7 g
Northstone Amber Ale	12 oz	13.5 g
Olde English 800	12 oz	10.5 g
Olde English 800 3.2	12 oz	6.9 g
Olde English 800 7.5	12 oz	13.1 g
Olde English 800 Ice	12 oz	14.3 g
Red Dog	12 oz	14.1 g
Sharp's	12 oz	12.1 g
SKYY Blue	12 oz	15 g
Southpaw Light	12 oz	6.3 g

Millstream

German Pilsner	12 oz	14.9 g
Schild Brau Amber	12 oz	16.8 g
Millstream Wheat	12 oz	11 g

Mishawaka

Founder's Stout	12 oz	11 g
Four Horsemen Irish Ale	12 oz	8 g
INDIAna Pale Ale	12 oz	9 g
Mishawaka Kolsch	12 oz	6 g
Raspberry Wheat	12 oz	7 g
Wall Street Wheat	12 oz	7 g

Molson

Canadian Lager	12 oz	12 g
Golden	12 oz	11.88 g
Molson Ice	12 oz	12 g
Molson Special Dry	12 oz	10 g
Ultra	12 oz	2.5 g

Murphy's

Murphy's Irish Red Beer	12 oz	8.82 g

New Belgium

1554	12 oz	24.9 g
Abbey	650 ml	15.99 g
Abbey Grand Cru	650 ml	17.7 g
Bier de Mars	12 oz	20.1 g
Blue Paddle	12 oz	16.7 g
Fat Tire	12 oz	17.7 g
Frambozen	12 oz	19.6 g
La Folie	750 ml	18.1 g

Loft	12 oz	9.9 g
Porch Swing	12 oz	12.49 g
Sunshine Wheat	12 oz	15.2 g
Transatlantique	12 oz	24.8 g
Trippel	12 oz	19.6 g

New Century

| Edison Light | 12 oz | 6.6 g |

New Glarus

| Spotted Cow | 12 oz | 13.56 g |

New Holland

Full Circle Single Malt	12 oz	14.75 g
Ichabod Pumpkin Ale	12 oz	17.75 g
Mad Hatter IPA	12 oz	16.7 g
Paleooza Pale Ale	12 oz	17.75 g
Poet Oatmeal Stout	12 oz	21.75 g
Sundog Amber	12 oz	17.75 g
Zoomer Wit	12 oz	15 g

Nor'Wester

Dunkel Weizen	12 oz	16.1 g
Hefeweizen	12 oz	12.6 g
Mt. Angel Oktoberfest	12 oz	23.7 g
OPA	12 oz	19.3 g
Raspberry Weizen	12 oz	12.6 g
Smith Rock Bock	12 oz	23.7 g

Oregon Ale and Beer

| ESB | 12 oz | 14.37 g |

Pabst

Ballantine Ale	12 oz	15.9 g
Blatz	12 oz	12.5 g
Blatz Light	12 oz	8.3 g
Carling Black Label	12 oz	12.5 g
Champale Extra Dry	12 oz	6.2 g
Champale Golden	12 oz	12.7 g
Colt 45	12 oz	11.1 g
Falstaff	12 oz	11.9 g
Heidelburg	12 oz	12.5 g
Kingsbury NA	12 oz	11.5 g
Lone Star	12 oz	11.4 g
Lone Star Light	12 oz	8.3 g
Lucky Lager	12 oz	11.9 g
McSorley's Ale	12 oz	15 g
McSorley's Black and Tan	12 oz	14.5 g
National Bohemian	12 oz	8.7 g
Old Milwaukee	12 oz	12.9 g
Old Milwaukee Light	12 oz	8.3 g
Old Style	12 oz	12 g
Old Style Light	12 oz	9.4 g
Olympia	12 oz	11.9 g
Pabst	12 oz	12.1 g
Pabst Light	12 oz	8.3 g
Pabst NA	12 oz	12 g
Pearl	12 oz	11.9 g
Piels	12 oz	8.7 g
Rainier	12 oz	11.4 g
Schaefer	12 oz	12 g
Schaefer's Light	12 oz	8.3 g
Schlitz	12 oz	12.1 g
Schmidts	12 oz	12.5 g

Special Export	12 oz	12.1 g
Stag	12 oz	12.5 g
St. Ides	12 oz	10.6 g
Stroh	12 oz	12 g
Stroh Light	12 oz	7 g

Pete's Wicked

Helles Lager	12 oz	14.6 g
Honey Wheat	12 oz	16.3 g
Oktoberfest	12 oz	16.5 g
Pub Lager	12 oz	14 g
Red Rush	12 oz	14.8 g
Signature Pilsner	12 oz	13.9 g
Strawberry Blonde	12 oz	13.7 g
Summer Brew	12 oz	14.2 g
Wicked Ale	12 oz	15.3 g
Winter Brew	12 oz	17.7 g

Pilsner Urquell

| Gambrinus | 12 oz | 9.8 g |
| Pilsner Urquell | 12 oz | 15.7 g |

Pittsburgh

American Light	12 oz	4.25 g
Augustiner	12 oz	10 g
Iron City	12 oz	10 g
Iron City Light	12 oz	2.8 g
Iron City Light Twist	12 oz	2.8 g

Pony Express

Gold Beer	12 oz	13.85 g
Original Wheat	12 oz	11.72 g
Rattlesnake Pale Ale	12 oz	13.85 g

Portland

Benchmark Old Ale	12 oz	32.1 g
Black Watch Cream Porter	12 oz	20.8 g
Bobby Dazzler Holiday Ale	12 oz	25.25 g
Highlander Pale	12 oz	17.3 g
Mac Frost	12 oz	23.25 g
MacTarnahan's Amber Ale	12 oz	18.5 g
Oregon Honey	12 oz	13.65 g
Otto's Weiss	12 oz	17.45 g
Portland Ale	12 oz	18.1 g
Uncle Otto's Oktoberfest	12 oz	23.7 g
Woodstock IPA	12 oz	20.35 g
Zig Zag River Lager	12 oz	18.2 g

Primus

Adler	12 oz	16.73 g
Charles Quint	12 oz	25.76 g
Primus	12 oz	13.55 g
Tongerlo Blonde 6	12 oz	20.09 g
Tongerlo Brune 6	12 oz	19.18 g
Tongerlo Triple 8	12 oz	13.37 g

Pyramid

Apricot Ale	12 oz	12.1 g
DPA	12 oz	15.25 g
Hefeweizen	12 oz	13 g
IPA	12 oz	21 g
Pale Ale	12 oz	15.25 g
Snowcap Ale	12 oz	22.5 g

ReaperAle (GreenFlash)

Deathly Pale Ale	12 oz	16.25 g
Mortality Stout	12 oz	24.1 g
Redemption Red Ale	12 oz	20.35 g

Redhook

Blonde	12 oz	13.13 g
Chinook Copper Ale	12 oz	14.63 g
ESB	12 oz	14.15 g
Sun Rye	12 oz	7.12 g
Black Hook Nitro	12 oz	12.92 g
Black Hook Porter	12 oz	12.92 g
Ballard Bitter (IPA)	12 oz	12.66 g
Hefeweissen	12 oz	10.58 g
IPA	12 oz	12.66 g
Nut Brown Ale	12 oz	16.02 g
Winter Hook (Seasonal Variations)	12 oz	15.54 g
Double Black Stout	12 oz	21.13 g

Richbrau

Big Nasty Porter	12 oz	10 g
Griffin Golden Ale	12 oz	10.4 g
Old Nick Pale Ale	12 oz	12.8 g

Sainsbury

Diät Pils	500 ml (½ liter)	2.85 g

Sapporo

Draft	12 oz	14 g

Sarapul's

Isetskoe	12 oz	20.59 g
Moskovskoe	12 oz	19.17 g
Leningradskoe	12 oz	27.34 g
Porter	12 oz	29.47 g
Martovskoe	12 oz	22.1 g
Rizhskoe	12 oz	17.4 g
Zhigulevskoe	12 oz	17.4 g
Dvoinoe Zolotoe	12 oz	20.59 g
Sarapulskoe	12 oz	20.59 g

Saxer

Bock	12 oz	23.8 g
Dark Bock	12 oz	19.3 g
Lemon Lager	12 oz	14.5 g
Pilsner	12 oz	15.3 g
Winter Doppelbock	12 oz	24.9 g

Sedona Beverages

Light Source	12 oz	2 g

Shipyard

Export Ale	12 oz	12 g
IPA	12 oz	13.33 g
Light	12 oz	7.4 g
Old Thumper	12 oz	13.7 g
Pumpkinhead Ale	12 oz	10.8 g
SeaDog Bluepaw	12 oz	10.8 g
Summer Ale	12 oz	12.2 g

Sierra Nevada

Bigfoot	12 oz	20–24.7 g
Pale Ale	12 oz	14.13 g
Porter	12 oz	18.39 g
Wheat	12 oz	13.09 g

Sinebrychoff, Russia

Koff I	12 oz	12 g
Koff III	12 oz	8.91 g
Koff IV A	12 oz	10.97 g
Koff IV B	12 oz	13.37 g
Koff Easter Beer III	12 oz	16.11 g
Special Strength Easter Beer	12 oz	12.68 g

Skagit River

Brown Ale	12 oz	16.6 g
Delrio American Lager	12 oz	9.95 g
Dutch Girl Lager	12 oz	13.4 g
Highwater Porter	12 oz	21.25 g
Huntsman (2003)	12 oz	16 g
Scullers	12 oz	17.5 g
Trumpeter Stout (2003)	12 oz	24.2 g
Washington's Wheat Ale	12 oz	13.5 g
Yellowjacket Pale Ale	12 oz	12.5 g

Sleeman

Sleeman Clear	12 oz	2.5 g

Smirnoff

Ice (malt-based)	12 oz	32 g

Snipes Mountain

American Hefeweizen	12 oz	14 g
Coyote Moon	12 oz	18 g
Extra Blonde Ale	12 oz	15 g
Harvest Ale	12 oz	18.5 g
IPA	12 oz	21 g
Porter	12 oz	21.3 g
Red Sky Ale	12 oz	19.75 g
Roza Reserve	12 oz	28.75 g
Sunnyside Pale Ale	12 oz	18.8 g

Somerfield

French Premier	12 oz	14.2 g
German Pilsner	12 oz	13.55 g

Spoetzl

Shiner Blond	12 oz	13 g
Shiner Bock	12 oz	12.5 g
Shiner Honey Wheat	12 oz	14.5 g
Shiner Light	12 oz	9 g
Shiner Summer Stock	12 oz	10.5 g
Shiner Winter Ale	12 oz	17.8 g

Sprecher

Abbey Triple	12 oz	22.45 g
Black Bavarian	12 oz	22 g
Hefe Weiss	12 oz	17.5 g
Pub Ale	12 oz	18.5 g
Special Amber	12 oz	17.75 g

Steinlager

Steinlager	12 oz	8.52 g
Steinlager (China)	12 oz	11.72 g

Straub

Straub	12 oz	10.5 g
Straub Light	12 oz	7.6 g

Swashbuckler

Lady Amber Ale	12 oz	14 g
Old Peg Leg Stout	12 oz	20.4 g
Rajah's Sword Pale Ale	12 oz	19.5 g
Scottland Strong Ale	12 oz	27 g
Swashbuckler's Gold	12 oz	12.6 g

Tesco

Organic Lager	12 oz	12.43 g
Premium Lager	12 oz	14.22 g
Value Lager	12 oz	4.26 g

Three Floyds

Alpha King	12 oz	22.9 g
Dreadnaught Imperial IPA	12 oz	32.1 g
Gumballhead	12 oz	21 g
Robert the Bruce	12 oz	21.7 g

Tinkoff, Russia — Draft

Pilsner	12 oz	18.82 g
Pilsner Filtered	12 oz	18.82 g
Lager	12 oz	20.59 g
Light	12 oz	16.33 g
Weissbier	12 oz	18.82 g

Tinkoff, Russia (continued)	Draft	
Porter	12 oz	21.69 g
Wheaten Porter	12 oz	20.24 g
Winter Bock	12 oz	28.76 g

Tinkoff, Russia	Bottled	
Bock	12 oz	21.3 g
Lager	12 oz	20.59 g
Pilsner	12 oz	18.82 g
Porter	12 oz	21.66 g
Weissbier	12 oz	18.82 g

Trailhead		
Missouri Brown Dark Ale	12 oz	19.75 g
Old Courthouse Dry Stout	12 oz	16.4 g
Riverboat Raspberry Fruit Ale	12 oz	14.4 g
Trailblazer Blonde Ale	12 oz	11.35 g
Trailhead Red Amber Ale	12 oz	18.9 g

Tsingtao		
Tsingtao	12 oz	12.5 g

Two Brothers		
Bitter End Pale Ale	12 oz	18.2 g
Ebel's Weiss	12 oz	14.5 g
Iditarod Imperial Stout	12 oz	21.25 g
Prairie Path Ale	12 oz	12.4 g

Upland		
Amber Ale	12 oz	19.8 g
Pale Ale	12 oz	18.5 g

Victory

Golden Monkey Tripel	12 oz	24 g
HopDevil	12 oz	21.4 g
Prima Pils	12 oz	16.3 g
Storm King Stout	12 oz	27.6 g

Warsteiner

Premium Fresh	12 oz	12.78 g
Premium Light	12 oz	8.16 g
Premium Verum	12 oz	10.6 g

Weihenstephan

Hefeweiss	12 oz	16.25 g
Hefeweiss Dunkel	12 oz	17 g
Hefeweiss Leicht	12 oz	11.25 g
Korbinian	12 oz	25.25 g
Kristall Weiss Bier	12 oz	16.25 g
Original	12 oz	13.75 g

Wellhead

Cisco Canyon Blonde	12 oz	14.1 g
Crude Oil Stout	12 oz	20 g
Indian Basin Wheat	12 oz	16.7 g
Pale Ale	12 oz	14.1 g
Roughneck Red	12 oz	17.7 g

Widmer Brothers

Blonde Ale	12 oz	9.6 g
Doppelbock	12 oz	20.8 g
Drop Top Amber Ale	12 oz	14.5 g
Hefe	12 oz	12.6 g
HopJack	12 oz	14.8 g

Widmer Brothers (continued)

Oktoberfest	12 oz	11.6 g
Sommerbrau	12 oz	10.8 g
SpringFest (Alt)	12 oz	13.6 g
Spring Run IPA	12 oz	16 g
Sweet Betty	12 oz	10.8 g
Widberry	12 oz	13 g
Wildwood Hard Cider	12 oz	21.8 g
Winternacht	12 oz	18.9 g

Young's

Chocolate Stout	12 oz	16.8 g
Dirty Dicks	12 oz	10.5 g
Export Lager	12 oz	7.7 g
Oatmeal Stout	12 oz	16.8 g
Old Nick	12 oz	35.7 g
Ram Rod	12 oz	12.25 g
Special London Ale	12 oz	19.25 g
Winter Warmer	12 oz	18.2 g

Yuengling

Premium	12 oz	12 g
Light	12 oz	6.6 g
Ale	12 oz	10 g
Porter	12 oz	14 g
Lager	12 oz	12 g
Black & Tan	12 oz	14 g

4

Ale-/Beer-Based Drinks

ONE OF THE MORE COMMON COMPLAINTS that some beer drinkers have with low-carb beers is the lack of flavor and body in the brew. By using these beers as a base for the following drinks, however, that perception falls to the wayside—with the added bonus of a low-carb drink delight. In order to standardize the following selection of ale- or beer-based drinks, I have used a typical low-carb beer with 5 grams of carbohydrates. Any exceptions are noted. You can make your own adjustments or substitutions as wanted and add to or subtract from the total carbohydrate count as listed with each drink recipe. Recipes for *Low-Carb Bartender* liqueurs used in some of these drinks can be found in Chapter 5.

Ale Flip

1 serving: 6.9 carbohydrates

What makes any drink a "flip" is the combination of egg, liquor, and sugar. The substitution of Splenda for sugar works well in any flip. The concept of eggs in mixed drinks, however, is a bit old-fashioned. I strongly suspect this is because of the fear of possible salmonella in raw eggs. However, pasteurized eggs, still in their shells, are becoming more common in grocery stores. Any of the popular containerized egg substitutes will work just as well.

12 ounces ale or beer
1 ounce white brandy
1 ounce lemon juice
2 teaspoons Splenda
1/8 teaspoon ground ginger
1 egg yolk, or 1 tablespoon egg substitute

Heat lemon juice, 2 ounces of ale or beer, ginger, and Splenda over moderate heat until thoroughly mixed.

Pour brandy into a bowl and add egg yolk from a pasteurized egg or 1 tablespoon of egg substitute.

Beat egg and brandy together. Slowly add heated mixture into bowl of egg and brandy while continuing to briskly beat egg yolk and brandy.

Pour contents of bowl into a beer mug and add rest of ale or beer. Stir.

Ale Sangaree
1 serving: 5.5 carbohydrates

A sangaree is actually a sweeter version of an Old-Fashioned. In this *LCB* version, you can enjoy it as is, or add a carb-free ounce of a distilled liquor such as whiskey, rum, or brandy to the drink for more kick and no additional carbohydrates.

½ teaspoon Splenda
12 ounces ale or beer
1 pinch nutmeg

In a beer mug, add Splenda and a bit of ale or beer to dissolve. Fill glass with ice. Top off with the rest of the ale or beer. Add a pinch of nutmeg to the foam.

Amber Beer Shot
1 serving: 2.10 carbohydrates

This drink substitutes the golden color of a typical light pilsner beer with a copper-colored Leinenkugel Amber Light. The amount of beer used in this drink even affords the opportunity to substitute higher-carbohydrate beers such as a high-octane bock beer. Not for the faint of heart!

1 ounce whiskey
1 ounce *LCB* Scotch Honey Whiskey
2 ounces Leinenkugel Amber Light

Fill an old-fashioned glass with ice. Pour in whiskey and *LCB* Scotch Honey Whiskey. Stir.

Top off with beer. Stir gently.

Beer Breezer
1 serving: 5 carbohydrates

The origin of this drink is uncertain, but it looks like another "cure" for a hangover. Even if you went a bit overboard the night before, this drink should help ease the pain and keep you in a *LCB* mode. Remember, though, drink responsibly and you'll never have this problem.

1 ounce vodka
12 ounces beer
2 dashes Tabasco sauce
1 pinch celery salt

Pour chilled vodka into a collins glass. Add the Tabasco sauce and celery salt. Top off with a cold beer. Stir slightly.

Beer Breezer II
1 serving: 3.65 carbohydrates

A totally different approach to the "therapeutic" one above but just as low-carb and tasty.

1 ounce lemon-flavored rum
1 ounce *LCB* Orange Liqueur
6 ounces beer
1 lemon slice

Fill an English pint glass with ice. Pour in rum and *LCB* Orange Liqueur. Stir. Pour in beer and stir gently.
Garnish with lemon slice.

Beer Buster
1 serving: 5 carbohydrates

Not sure if it's the vodka or the Tabasco sauce that "busts" the beer in this drink, but the inclusion of both puts zip into any low-carb or light beer choice.

1 ounce vodka
12 ounces beer
1 dash Tabasco sauce

Pour vodka into a pilsner glass. Top off with ice-cold beer. Add dash of Tabasco sauce.

Beer Colada
1 serving: 5.5 carbohydrates

The carbonation from the beer subtly mutes the inherent sweetness found in the colada mix.

4 ounces Baja Bob's Pina Colada Mix
1 ounce dark rum
1 tablespoon Da Vinci Sugar Free Banana Syrup
6 ounces beer
1 orange slice (thin)

Half-fill a shaker with ice.

Pour in all ingredients except beer. Shake and strain into a hurricane glass, filled with crushed ice.

Pour in beer and stir gently. Garnish with a thin slice of orange.

Berliner Weisse

1 serving: 8.25 carbohydrates

The combination of an unfiltered wheat beer and a shot of fruit-flavored syrup is a popular drink in Berlin. It's typically served in a fishbowl-shaped schooner, a huge beer glass that was popular in American saloons before National Prohibition. I used a Widmer Brothers Hefe wheat beer with only 12.6 carbohydrates in a 12-ounce serving.

6 ounces wheat beer
½ ounce *LCB* Strawberry Liqueur

Pour *LCB* Strawberry Liqueur into a smaller-sized brandy snifter. Top off with wheat beer. Gently swirl and enjoy.

Black & Tan

1 serving: 4.8 carbohydrates

Depending on whom you talk to, the original Black & Tan consisted of Bass Ale and Guinness Stout. Go with a Bass Ale instead of a 5-carb light beer and add 8 more carbohydrates to the total below. If you want to go all-Guinness with this drink, a Harp Lager will also add an additional 8 carbs to the total. The name "Black & Tan" supposedly refers to the color of the uniform worn by English police recruited for duty on the Emerald Isle during the early 1900s.

6 ounces beer
6 ounces Guinness Draught

Pour equal amounts of both beers into a beer stein or an English pint glass.

Black Velvet

1 serving: 8.6 carbohydrates

Don't use a light beer for this recipe. Without Guinness, it's not a Black Velvet, just a beer and champagne mixed drink.

6 ounces Guinness Draught
6 ounces champagne

Pour equal amounts of Guinness and champagne into a beer stein or an English pint glass.

Boilermaker

1 serving: 5 carbohydrates

The workingman's drink. Quick, neat, efficient—and low-carb!

1 ounce whiskey
12 ounces beer

Pour whiskey into a pilsner glass. Top off with beer.

Cincinnati

1 serving: 1.66 carbohydrates

If you're really going tight with the carbs today, this might be the way to go.

4 ounces beer
4 ounces seltzer or soda water

In a highball glass, pour in beer. Top off with seltzer or soda water.

Demi Panache, Shandy, or Radler

1 serving: 4 carbohydrates

Being more of a beer drinker, I wasn't sure if I'd like this blend. I mixed my first Shandy with Minute-Maid Light Lemonade (3 carbs in a 12-ounce can) and found the drink to be a nice summertime *LCB* alternative to simply quaffing a cold beer. Shandys are very popular in Europe, especially with younger drinkers. In Germany, this drink is known as a Radler.

6 ounces beer
6 ounces diet lemonade (or diet lemon-lime soda)

Pour 6 ounces of beer and 6 ounces of diet lemonade into a chilled pilsner glass.

Depth Charge

1 serving: 12.4 carbohydrates

Substitute 1 ounce of vodka and 1 teaspoon of Da Vinci Peppermint Paddy Sugar Free Syrup for the peppermint schapps and save 7.4 carbs total. Remember, use your imagination and a good dose of creativity when putting on your *Low-Carb Bartender* apron!

12 ounces beer
1 ounce peppermint schnapps

Pour beer into a pint glass. Carefully drop in a shot glass filled with schnapps.

Dive Bomber
1 serving: 5.9 carbohydrates

Recipe ideas for making *Low-Carb Bartender* liqueurs used in this drink can be found in Chapter 5.

⅓ ounce *LCB* Amaretto
⅔ ounce *LCB* Root Beer Schnapps
12 ounces beer

Fill 1-ounce shot glass with mixture of *LCB* Amaretto and *LCB* Root Beer Schnapps.

Fill a beer mug or English pint glass with beer.

Carefully drop shot glass into beer and drink before it fizzes over the top of the glass.

Dog's Nose
1 serving: 5 carbohydrates

An old English beer cocktail that was mentioned in *The Pickwick Papers* by Charles Dickens. Dickens obviously wasn't counting carbs since his version included brown sugar. If you have it on hand, add a pinch or two of Sugar Twin brown sugar to this drink for more authenticity.

1 ounce gin
12 ounces beer or ale

Pour gin and then beer or ale into a pint glass.

L. G. Cocktail
1 serving: 5 carbohydrates

Whereas a boilermaker consists of whiskey and beer, a shot of Scotch, especially a single-malt Scotch, makes this a nice high-class variation of an old workingman's drink.

1 ounce Scotch
12 ounces beer

Either pour Scotch into a pilsner glass and add beer or simply throw back the Scotch with beer as a chaser.

Red Eye
1 serving: 10.5 carbohydrates

Not as bad as it sounds, especially as a hangover cure.

6 ounces beer
6 ounces tomato juice

Pour beer and tomato juice into a beer mug. Stir carefully.

Skip and Go Naked
1 serving: 6.5 carbohydrates

. . . go naked? Don't you dare!

1 ounce gin
1 ounce Baja Bob's Sweet-n-Sour Mix
12 ounces beer
1 dash *LCB* grenadine syrup

Add all ingredients to a beer mug or English pint glass. Stir gently.

Weissbeer Mojito

1 serving: 7 carbohydrates

Talk about a cultural clash! The use of a German/American-styled wheat beer in this typically Cuban drink takes advantage of the inherent spiciness and banana flavors from the yeast used in wheat beers. I used American Wheat "312" brand from the Goose Island Brewery in Chicago for its spiciness and very manageable carbohydrate count of only 10.5 grams in a 12-ounce serving.

1 ounce dark rum
1 teaspoon Splenda
1 tablespoon lime juice
3 mint leaves
6 ounces wheat beer
1 mint sprig

Muddle (grind together) mint leaves and Splenda in an English pint glass with a bar spoon.

Pour in rum and lime juice. If using a fresh lime, toss in shell of the lime. Fill with ice and stir.

Top off with wheat beer and stir gently. Garnish with mint sprig.

5

Making *Low-Carb Bartender* Liqueurs and Cordials

MANY OF THE STORE-BOUGHT LIQUEURS and cordials listed in Chapter 1 can be enjoyed in moderation by *LCB* customers in the later stages of a low-carbohydrate diet or by those who have reached their target weight and are now in any sort of weight maintenance phase. There are recipes online and in numerous books, however, for making home-made liqueurs that can be tweaked into low-carbohydrate drink delights and enjoyed by any *Low-Carb Bartender* customer during almost every stage of their diet.

The key "ingredients" in these recipes are time and patience. Unfortunately, one doesn't always have the luxury of these two elements. The secret to making good quality, low-carb liqueurs—and in a timely fashion—begins with liqueur extracts, a popular item in some European countries where government taxation on alcohol-based products can be excessive. This has created a thriving industry of liqueur extracts manufacturers and hundreds of recipes for making cordials and apéritifs. I'll begin with a few recipes that include real ingredients—a true home-made effort—and then move on to simpler liqueur recipes using liqueur essences. Consider these different routes in making liqueurs similar to baking a cake (a low-carb cake, of course!). With a cake, you could simply make one from a package mix and immediately enjoy your effort, or compile all the separate ingredients yourself and make your own. The time and effort you save by using a package mix might be—or might not be—worth the extra effort and time that it takes to create a homemade cake or a low-carb liqueur—it's your call.

When choosing a base for homemade liqueurs, it's often suggested that you buy the cheapest brand of vodka, brandy, whiskey, rum, or whatever liquor you might need or want to use as a base. I don't necessarily subscribe to this opinion. In the case of vodka-based liqueurs, however, I've found it much cheaper and more accurate to use grain alcohol in achieving the correct proof of the liqueur. Vodka is, after all, a clear, neutral spirit that has been blended with water to bring down its alcoholic strength. Everclear, probably the most popular brand of grain alcohol, is 95% pure, odorless, and virtually tasteless, with a proof of 190°. This is not the sort of drink that you should pour out in its high-concentrate strength for knocking back shots or simply to sip on. You're more likely to find grain alcohol at a larger liquor store than at a neighborhood one.

When adding extracts, essences, herbs, or flavorings to your *LCB* liqueurs, go for the best ingredients you can find.

Equipment

You might already have most of the equipment needed to make *LCB* liqueurs at home. You'll find information on where you can purchase extracts, glycerin, and equipment in the Appendix.

Bottles

I like to use decorative quart-sized bottles with ceramic and rubber gasket flippy stoppers. You can find these at stores like Target, K-Mart, Ikea, or Crate & Barrel.

Canning Jars

For mixing and mellowing purposes, a few 32- and 64-ounce canning jars with lids can be used.

Cheesecloth

Use cheesecloth in a metal colander for the primary straining of liqueurs, especially if making a fruit-based drink. Once the *LCB* liqueur is cleaned of larger sediment, use conical coffee filters in a small funnel to brighten the product.

Coffee Filters

Use the conical ones that will fit into a funnel. After straining *LCB* liqueurs with the cheesecloth/colander setup, the liquid will eventually clear as the flavorings and smaller ingredients drop to the bottom of the mixing container. Coffee filters will help clear (brighten) your *LCB* liqueurs before a final bottling. Filtering your *LCB* liqueurs takes a bit of time and patience but you'll be rewarded with clear and brilliant drinks.

Colander

Use in conjunction with cheesecloth to remove visible particulates in your *LCB* liqueurs. Use a metal colander, as plastic can retain unwanted flavors and impart them to your *LCB* liqueurs.

Distilled Water

Use distilled water when you prepare your liqueur—you don't want the taste or smell of chlorine or minerals to come through the flavor of the liqueur.

Funnel

Use a plastic or stainless steel funnel. If you're going to use a plastic funnel, put it away afterward and don't use it for anything else, especially greasy or highly-flavored liquids. Make sure the nozzle will fit comfortably into your bottles. The first time you go to buy coffee filters, take the funnel with you and try to gauge whether or not the filters will fit into the funnel. And no, I'm not telling you to open packages of filters in the supermarket aisle.

Glycerin

You can skip the glycerin if you want, but the use of artifical sweeteners limits the viscosity, or thickness, of the liqueur. Glycerin (also known as glycerine or glycerol) is used in a number of low-carb foods to add depth and richness. Some manufacturers of these foods like to ignore a Food and Drug Administration ruling that glycerin is a carbohydrate and that it must be added to total carb counts in food. They are now being confronted with the might of the federal government. I have included glycerin as an element of the total carbohydrate count for the

following liqueur recipes. There are 34.7 grams of carbohydrates in 1 fluid ounce of glycerin. I use 1 to 2 tablespoons of glycerin in my *LCB* liqueurs, depending on the
viscosity of the original product. For a 2-tablespoon (1-
ounce) dosage in 28 ounces of *LCB* Amaretto, for
instance, you're only adding about 1.24 additional carbs
to a 1-ounce serving.

Labels

You can add a decorative touch to your labels with a
number of cheap software programs that allow you to cus-
tomize bottle labels to whatever specifications you desire.
Aside from the name of the liqueur, I also like to add the
date of bottling. Adding the "vintage" date can give you a
better idea of how much smoother the liqueur can become
as it ages, something you might want to remember when
you make another batch.

Stainless Steel Pot

Some liqueur recipes call for fruit and can't be accom-
modated in a quart-sized glass canning jar. You can find
cheap stainless steelware with lids at department stores
like Target or K-Mart.

Low-Carb Bartender Blueberry Liqueur

Approximately 28 1-ounce servings:
2.85 carbohydrates per serving

The carb count of this product is "guesstimated" using the original carbohydrate counts of the blueberries and raspberries. Although the spent berries are disposed of and not eaten, I've nonetheless calculated the carbs per serving using the higher number.

1 cup Splenda
6 ounces grain alcohol
20 ounces distilled water
2 cups fresh (or frozen) red raspberries
1 cup fresh (or frozen) blueberries
1 tablespoon real vanilla extract
1 tablespoon glycerin

Combine Splenda and raspberries/blueberries in a large mixing bowl and muddle them together until the berries have broken open.

Pour this mixture into a quart-sized canning jar. Pour in grain alcohol, water, and vanilla extract. Cover with lid. Shake.

Store in cool, dark place for 2 months (refrigerator is okay). Gently shake jar twice a week.

After 2 months, strain through cheesecloth draped in a metal colander and placed in a large bowl. Pour liqueur into another quart-sized canning jar. Dispose of berries.

After 1 additional month of storage, strain liqueur into decorative quart-sized bottle using a funnel lined with a conical coffee filter. Add glycerin. Shake.

Label and date the liqueur. Store in a dark place for at least 1 month.

Low-Carb Bartender **Mexican Coffee Liqueur**

Approximately 28 1-ounce servings:
2.96 carbohydrates per serving

This recipe emulates a low-carb version of Kahlúa. It's great poured on LC vanilla ice cream.

2 cups Splenda
6 ounces grain alcohol
20 ounces distilled water
⅜ cup instant coffee granules
1 tablespoon vanilla extract
1 tablespoon glycerin

Combine all ingredients except glycerin in a quart-sized canning jar.

Shake jar until coffee granules are dissolved. Store liqueur in a sealed glass canning jar for 1 week.

Using a small funnel lined with a conical coffee filter, transfer the strained mixture into a decorative quart-sized bottle. Add glycerin. Shake.

Label and date the liqueur. Store in a cool, dark place for at least 1 week.

Low-Carb Bartender Cranberry Liqueur
Approximately 28 1-ounce servings:
4.25 carbohydrates per serving

The carb counts in this recipe are calculated as though the cranberries are actually consumed.

4 cups fresh (or frozen) whole cranberries,
coarsely chopped
2 cups Splenda
1 tablespoon lemon juice
6 ounces grain alcohol
20 ounces distilled water
1 tablespoon glycerin

In a large stainless steel pot with lid, combine cranberries, Splenda, lemon juice, grain alcohol, and water.

Stir contents until Splenda is dissolved. Cover liquid with lid. Allow mixture to stand at room temperature for 2 weeks, stirring every day.

After 2 weeks, strain liqueur through cheesecloth draped in a metal colander and placed in a large bowl. Pour strained liqueur into another quart-sized canning jar. Dispose of cranberries.

After 1 month, strain into decorative quart-sized bottle using a funnel lined with a conical coffee filter. Add glycerin. Shake.

Label and date the liqueur. Store in a dark place for at least 1 month.

Low-Carb Bartender Strawberry Liqueur

Approximately 28 1-ounce servings:

3.88 carbohydrates per serving

For this recipe, you could just as easily substitute raspberries for the strawberries and make a *LCB* Framboise.

4 cups very ripe strawberries
1 tablespoon real vanilla extract
1¾ cup Splenda
10 ounces grain alcohol
16 ounces distilled water
1 tablespoon glycerin

Cut off stems and any green parts of the strawberries. Lightly rinse them. Slice the strawberries and put them in a large stainless steel pot with a lid. Add all the other ingredients except glycerin.

Put lid on pot and soak the strawberries for a month, gently stirring them once or twice a day.

When you have finished steeping the mixture, remove the strawberries by placing a colander into a large bowl and gently pouring the liqueur through the colander lined with cheesecloth.

Pour the partially cleared liqueur into a quart-sized canning jar. Put on lid and tighten. Let the *LCB* liqueur sit for 2 weeks.

After 2 weeks, strain into a decorative quart-sized bottle using a funnel lined with a conical coffee filter. Add glycerin. Shake.

Label and date the liqueur. Store in a dark place for at least 1 month.

Low-Carb Bartender Limoncello

Makes approximately 2 quarts
(approximately 64 1-ounce servings).
1.70 carbohydrates per serving

This is the most work-intensive *LCB* liqueur recipe in this section and requires the most time to settle and mellow—but boy is it good. Treat this with kid gloves since it runs about 95 proof!

12 thick-skinned lemons
One 750 ml bottle of grain alcohol
4½ cups Splenda
4 cups distilled water

Wash and scrub lemons in hot water. Remove the peel with a vegetable peeler, being careful to avoid peeling the white pith—it will give the limoncello a bitter taste.

If necessary, scrape pith from peels with a knife. Put the peels in a large stainless steel pot with lid.

Add ½ bottle of grain alcohol and 2 cups of water and close the lid. Date the pot, and put it to rest in a dark space at room temperature for 4 weeks.

After 4 weeks, open up the mixture. In a saucepan, stir Splenda and one cup of distilled water together and lightly simmer for one minute.

Let the Splenda syrup cool completely in the pan—about 5 minutes. Add Splenda syrup to the lemon/grain alcohol/water mixture in the stainless steel pot. Top off with the rest of the grain alcohol and 1 more cup of distilled water.

Stir and close the lid. Date the mixture for another 30 days. Return mixture to a dark space.

At the end of those 30 days, strain the mixture using a metal colander draped with cheesecloth and placed in a large bowl. Discard the lemon peels. Pour liquid into 2 decorative quart-sized bottles using a funnel lined with a conical coffee filter to brighten the liqueur.

Label and date the *LCB* Limoncello. Store in a dark place for at least 1 month. Put 1 bottle at a time in the freezer, if desired.

As you can see, there can be a period of weeks, if not months, before many of these homemade *LCB* liqueurs are ready for enjoyment. As great as they taste, we can't always sit around waiting to enjoy them (though once you get an adequate supply built up, you'll have time to make more at your own leisure).

If your time is limited for experimentation, let me suggest Liquor Quik essences from the Winemakeri company as a quicker and tasty alternative to the recipes above. These essences are concentrated flavorings that emulate the taste of a number of commercial liqueurs. A check of their ingredients listed on the .65-fluid ounce (20 ml) bottles include natural extracts, essences, oils, and sometimes caramel color. I contacted Michael Oxner at Winemakeri, Inc. *(www.winemakeri.com)* who assured me that " There are no nutritional values associated with essential oil-based essences such as our brand." Not that I didn't believe him, but I did do a test for glucose after adding the alcohol to a mixture of each of the following essences and water. I did this before adding Splenda, which uses dextrose (glucose) and maltodextrin as a base for pourability and boosts the Splenda product to 24 carbohydrates per 8-ounce cup. All the essence/grain alcohol/water solutions came up negative for glucose.

The recipes included with Liquor Quik essences are normally sweetened by adding white cane sugar to a mixture of distilled water, the Liquor Quik essence, alcohol, and some glycerin to firm up the body of the liqueur, if needed. This glycerin addition is, I think, essential when substituting Splenda in the recipes for cane sugar, since sugar gives the liqueurs the kind of viscosity that you won't get with Splenda. As mentioned before, I calculate 2 tablespoons of glycerin to equal 1 fluid ounce, which equals 34.7 carbohydrates. Liquor Quik recommends adding 1 ounce of glycerin in their recipes, but I've often halved this to 1 tablespoon with only 17.35 carbohydrates. Diluted to a final product of about 28 ounces brings this number down to an almost negligible amount of carbs per serving. You can always skip the addition of glycerin to your *LCB* liqueurs if desired, but the liqueur will be thin-bodied. At times, I actually pour in a 1-ounce portion (2 tablespoons) for additional thickness in the liqueur and adjust the total carbohydrate count accordingly. This is simply a matter of taste.

Just to give you an idea of the simplicity of the use of these products, following is a typical *Low-Carb Bartender* liqueur recipe interpretation using these Liquor Quik essences. A list of flavors that are currently available from the Winemakeri company is also included with suggested low-carb recipes.

Low-Carb Bartender Amaretto
Approximately 28 1-ounce servings:
2.52 carbohydrates per serving

Amaretto Di Saronno is probably the best known brand of this almond-like liqueur. It has a proof of 56°, or 28% alcohol. Hiram Walker also makes this liqueur with a proof of 50°, or 25% alcohol. Through experience and personal taste, I have slightly adjusted the liquids used to yield about 26 to 28 fluid ounces of finished product—your mileage may vary. The manufacturer's recipe comes in at a suggested yield of 31 fluid ounces. Two reasons for my tweaking of the recipe: First, I find my interpretation gives a bit more flavor intensity to the *LCB* liqueur; and second, all I had on hand were decorative bottles that hold a little more than 28 ounces.

1 bottle Liquor Quik Amaretto
6 ounces grain alcohol
20 ounces distilled water
1¼ cups Splenda
1 tablespoon glycerin

Add all ingredients except glycerin to a clean 32-ounce canning jar. Close lid and shake for a good 10 seconds.

Let the *LCB* Amaretto sit in a dark place for 1 week. Line a funnel with a conical coffee filter and pour the *LCB* Amaretto into a decorative quart-sized bottle. Add glycerin. Shake for a few seconds.

Label and date the liqueur. Store in a dark place for at least 1 week.

Liquor Quik Essences

The recipes for the other Liquor Quik essences are similar in formula. As with the *LCB* Amaretto recipe above, use 6 ounces of grain alcohol, 20 ounces of distilled water and the appropriate amount of Splenda as your template for the following *LCB* liqueur recipes. Note that the amount of Splenda varies according to the sweetness profile of the real liqueur.

I make an effort to come close to the percentage of alcohol or the proof of the original liqueur. That's why I like using grain alcohol. I start with the idea that I am looking for an initial target of 26 ounces. Volume displacement from the Splenda will push it up a few more ounces. My "guesstimate" is a volume target of 26 to 28 ounces.

So, in a nutshell, if you take 26 ounces and want a finished product with a proof of 50°, remember that proof is represented by two times the actual alcohol content, or conversely, alcohol content equals one-half the stated proof. In the case of 50 proof, you will need 25% of the 26 fluid ounces to consist of grain alcohol. Simply multiply 26 by .25 and you arrive at 6.5 ounces of alcohol. Now this isn't rocket science, so if I don't quite hit a whole number, I normally round down—in other words, since the calculation above gave me 6.5 ounces of grain alcohol, I'd use 6 ounces. Going back to the original calculation of 26 ounces times .25 (or 50 proof), add 20 ounces of distilled water to the 6 ounces of grain alcohol and you have about 26 to 28 ounces of a solution that approximates 50-proof.

Anisette (Pastis)

Approximately 28 1-ounce servings:

1.50 carbohydrates per serving

A sweet, anise seed–flavored liqueur that emulsifies (becomes milky) when mixed with water.

> 1 bottle Liquor Quik Anisette
> 6 ounces grain alcohol
> 20 ounces distilled water
> 1 cup Splenda
> 1 tablespoon glycerin

Add all ingredients except glycerin to a clean 32-ounce canning jar. Close lid and shake for a good 10 seconds.

Let the *LCB* Anisette sit in a dark place for 1 week. Line a funnel with a conical coffee filter and pour the *LCB* Anisette into a decorative quart-sized bottle. Add glycerin. Shake for a few seconds.

Label and date the liqueur. Store in a dark place for at least 1 week.

Apricot Brandy
Approximately 28 1-ounce servings:
1.5 carbohydrates per serving

A blend of brandy and apricots.

1 bottle Liquor Quik Apricot Brandy
6 ounces grain alcohol
20 ounces distilled water
1 cup Splenda
1 tablespoon glycerin

Add all ingredients except glycerin to a clean 32-ounce canning jar. Close lid and shake for a good 10 seconds.

Let the *LCB* Apricot Brandy sit in a dark place for 1 week. Line a funnel with a conical coffee filter and pour the *LCB* Apricot Brandy into a decorative quart-sized bottle. Add glycerin. Shake for a few seconds.

Label and date the liqueur. Store in a dark place for at least 1 week.

Caribbean Coffee
Approximately 28 1-ounce servings:
1.50 carbohydrates per serving

A Jamaican coffee liqueur with coffee beans and rum.

1 bottle Liquor Quik Caribbean Coffee
6 ounces grain alcohol
20 ounces distilled water
1 cup Splenda
1 tablespoon glycerin

Add all ingredients except glycerin to a clean 32-ounce canning jar. Close lid and shake for a good 10 seconds.

Let the *LCB* Caribbean Coffee sit in a dark place for 1 week. Line a funnel with a conical coffee filter and pour the *LCB* Caribbean Coffee into a decorative quart-sized bottle. Add glycerin. Shake for a few seconds.

Label and date the liqueur. Store in a dark place for at least 1 week.

Coconut Rum

Approximately 28 1-ounce servings:
1.50 carbohydrates per serving

A blend of coconut and white rum.

1 bottle Liquor Quik Coconut Rum
12 ounces grain alcohol
14 ounces distilled water
1 cup Splenda
1 tablespoon glycerin

Add all ingredients except glycerin to a clean 32-ounce canning jar. Close lid and shake for a good 10 seconds.

Let the *LCB* Coconut Rum sit in a dark place for 1 week. Line a funnel with a conical coffee filter and pour the *LCB* Coconut Rum into a decorative quart-sized bottle. Add glycerin. Shake for a few seconds.

Label and date the liqueur. Store in a dark place for at least 1 week.

Crème de Menthe

Approximately 28 1-ounce servings:
1.9 carbohydrates per serving

The classic green peppermint liqueur.

1 bottle Liquor Quik Crème de Menthe
6 ounces grain alcohol
20 ounces distilled water
1¼ cups Splenda
1 tablespoon glycerin

Add all ingredients except glycerin to a clean 32-ounce canning jar. Close lid and shake for a good 10 seconds.

Let the *LCB* Crème de Menthe sit in a dark place for 1 week. Line a funnel with a conical coffee filter and pour the *LCB* Crème de Menthe into a decorative quart-sized bottle. Add glycerin. Shake for a few seconds.

Label and date the liqueur. Store in a dark place for at least 1 week.

Hazelnut

Approximately 28 1-ounce servings:
1.9 carbohydrates per serving

A traditional Italian nut liqueur.

1 bottle Liquor Quik Hazelnut
6 ounces grain alcohol
20 ounces distilled water
1¼ cups Splenda
1 tablespoon glycerin

Add all ingredients except glycerin to a clean 32-ounce canning jar. Close lid and shake for a good 10 seconds.

Let the *LCB* Hazelnut sit in a dark place for 1 week. Line a funnel with a conical coffee filter and pour the *LCB* Hazelnut into a decorative quart-sized bottle. Add glycerin. Shake for a few seconds.

Label and date the liqueur. Store in a dark place for at least 1 week.

Irish Cream

Approximately 28 1-ounce servings:
2.5 carbohydrates per serving

A blend of Irish Whisky, cream, and chocolate. This essence is an amazing product.

1 bottle Liquor Quik Irish Cream
6 ounces grain alcohol
20 ounces distilled water
1 cup Splenda

Add all ingredients to a clean 32-ounce canning jar. Close lid and shake for a good 10 seconds.

Let the *LCB* Irish Cream sit in a dark place for 1 week. Line a funnel with a conical coffee filter and pour the *LCB* Irish Cream into a decorative quart-sized bottle. Do *not* add glycerin. Shake for a few seconds.

Label and date the liqueur. Store in a dark place for at least 1 week.

Before serving, add 1 ounce of heavy or whipping cream to 1 ounce of the *LCB* Irish Cream and stir together in a glass with some ice cubes for a few seconds. Voilà!

Italiano

Approximately 28 1-ounce servings:
1.5 carbohydrates per serving

A popular Italian herb and vanilla liqueur.

1 bottle Liquor Quik Italiano
6 ounces grain alcohol
20 ounces distilled water
1 cup Splenda
1 tablespoon glycerin

Add all ingredients except glycerin to a clean 32-ounce canning jar. Close lid and shake for a good 10 seconds.

Let the *LCB* Italiano sit in a dark place for 1 week. Line a funnel with a conical coffee filter and pour the *LCB* Italiano into a decorative quart-sized bottle. Add glycerin. Shake for a few seconds.

Label and date the liqueur. Store in a dark place for at least 1 week.

Mexican Coffee

Approximately 28 1-ounce servings:
1.5 carbohydrates per serving

Emulates the world's number-one coffee liqueur.

1 bottle Liquor Quik Mexican Coffee
6 ounces grain alcohol
20 ounces distilled water
1 cup Splenda
1 tablespoon glycerin

Add all ingredients except glycerin to a clean 32-ounce canning jar. Close lid and shake for a good 10 seconds.

Let the *LCB* Mexican Coffee sit in a dark place for 1 week. Line a funnel with a conical coffee filter and pour the *LCB* Mexican Coffee into a decorative quart-sized bottle. Add glycerin. Shake for a few seconds.

Label and date the liqueur. Store in a dark place for at least 1 week.

Orange Brandy
Approximately 28 1-ounce servings:
1.15 carbohydrates per serving

A blend of orange and brandy.

1 bottle Liquor Quik Orange Brandy
6 ounces grain alcohol
20 ounces distilled water
¾ cup Splenda
1 tablespoon glycerin

Add all ingredients except glycerin to a clean 32-ounce canning jar. Close lid and shake for a good 10 seconds.

Let the *LCB* Orange Brandy sit in a dark place for 1 week. Line a funnel with a conical coffee filter and pour the *LCB* Orange Brandy into a decorative quart-sized bottle. Add glycerin. Shake for a few seconds.

Label and date the liqueur. Store in a dark place for at least 1 week.

Peach Schnapps

Approximately 28 1-ounce servings:

1.5 carbohydrates per serving

A classic fruit liqueur.

1 bottle Liquor Quik Peach Schnapps
6 ounces grain alcohol
20 ounces distilled water
1 cup Splenda
1 tablespoon glycerin

Add all ingredients except glycerin to a clean 32-ounce canning jar. Close lid and shake for a good 10 seconds.

Let the *LCB* Peach Schnapps sit in a dark place for 1 week. Line a funnel with a conical coffee filter and pour the *LCB* Schnapps into a decorative quart-sized bottle. Add glycerin. Shake for a few seconds.

Label and date the liqueur. Store in a dark place for at least 1 week.

Sambuca

Approximately 28 1-ounce servings:

1.15 carbohydrates per serving

A popular Italian anise seed (licorice-tasting) liqueur.

1 bottle Liquor Quik Sambuca
6 ounces grain alcohol
20 ounces distilled water
¾ cup Splenda
1 tablespoon glycerin

Add all ingredients except glycerin to a clean 32-ounce canning jar. Close lid and shake for a good 10 seconds.

Let the *LCB* Sambuca sit in a dark place for 1 week. Line a funnel with a conical coffee filter and pour the *LCB* Sambuca into a decorative quart-sized bottle. Add glycerin. Shake for a few seconds.

Label and date the liqueur. Store in a dark place for at least 1 week.

Scotch Honey Whisky
Approximately 28 1-ounce servings:
1.70 carbohydrates per serving

A famous blend of whisky, honey, and herbs.

1 bottle Liquor Quik Scotch Honey Whisky
6 ounces grain alcohol
20 ounces distilled water
1¼ cups Splenda
1 tablespoon glycerin

Add all ingredients except glycerin to a clean 32-ounce canning jar. Close lid and shake for a good 10 seconds.

Let the *LCB* Scotch Honey Whisky sit in a dark place for 1 week. Line a funnel with a conical coffee filter and pour the *LCB* Scotch Honey Whisky into a decorative quart-sized bottle. Add glycerin. Shake for a few seconds.

Label and date the liqueur. Store in a dark place for at least 1 week.

Southern Whiskey

Approximately 28 1-ounce servings:

1.05 carbohydrates per serving

A delicious blend of bourbon whiskey and citrus fruits.

1 bottle Liquor Quik Southern Whiskey

12 ounces grain alcohol

14 ounces distilled water

½ cup Splenda

1 tablespoon glycerin

Add all ingredients except glycerin to a clean 32-ounce canning jar. Close lid and shake for a good 10 seconds.

Let the *LCB* Southern Whiskey sit in a dark place for 1 week. Line a funnel with a conical coffee filter and pour the *LCB* Southern Whiskey into a decorative quart-sized bottle. Add glycerin. Shake for a few seconds.

Label and date the liqueur. Store in a dark place for at least 1 week.

Swiss Chocolate Almond

Approximately 28 1-ounce servings:

1.7 carbohydrates per serving

A delicious blend of dark chocolate and almond.

1 bottle Liquor Quik Swiss Chocolate Almond

6 ounces grain alcohol

20 ounces distilled water

1¼ cups Splenda

1 tablespoon glycerin

Add all ingredients except glycerin to a clean 32-ounce canning jar. Close lid and shake for a good 10 seconds.

Let the *LCB* Swiss Chocolate Almond sit in a dark place for 1 week. Line a funnel with a conical coffee filter and pour the *LCB* Swiss Chocolate Almond into a decorative quart-sized bottle. Add glycerin. Shake for a few seconds.

Label and date the liqueur. Store in a dark place for at least 1 week.

Triple Sec
Approximately 28 1-ounce servings:
1.5 carbohydrates per serving

A citrus liqueur made from brandy, orange peel, and herbs.

1 bottle Liquor Quik Triple Sec
6 ounces grain alcohol
20 ounces distilled water
1 cup Splenda
1 tablespoon glycerin

Add all ingredients except glycerin to a clean 32-ounce canning jar. Close lid and shake for a good 10 seconds.

Let the *LCB* Triple Sec sit in a dark place for 1 week. Line a funnel with a conical coffee filter and pour the *LCB* Triple Sec into a decorative quart-sized bottle. Add glycerin. Shake for a few seconds.

Label and date the liqueur. Store in a dark place for at least 1 week.

McCormick Extracts

There's also a company that makes a line of 1-ounce extracts that are available in almost any grocery store— McCormick *(www.mccormick.com)*. Though I try to keep away from imitation extracts, they do have a number of pure extracts that deserve the attention of any adventurous LC dieter who might want to expand his or her own inventory of *LCB* liqueurs. The pure extracts are:

- Pure Mint Extract (Think clear Crème de Menthe or peppermint schnapps)
- Pure Orange Extract (Orange-flavored vodka or, if added to cognac, perhaps a Grand Marnier–type liqueur)
- Pure Lemon Extract (Lemon-flavored vodka or Limoncello)
- Pure Anise Extract (Sambuca)
- Pure Almond Extract (Amaretto)

They also manufacture imitation flavored extracts. They are:

- Imitation Pineapple Extract
- Imitation Coconut Extract (Add the pineapple and coconut to rum for a Caribbean-style rum)
- Imitation Cherry Extract (Cherry schnapps)
- Imitation Banana Extract (Banana schnapps)
- Imitation Strawberry Extract (Fragolo)

Though you may want to stay away from using imitation flavorings whenever possible, these might be worth a good hard look for making *LCB* liqueurs.

Low-Carb Bartender Root Beer Schnapps

Approximately 28 1-ounce servings:
1.7 carbohydrates per serving

Not an extract but a concentrate, the 2-ounce bottle of Root Beer Concentrate can be used to make root beer schnapps. On the McCormick Web site, both the pure and imitation extracts and the root beer concentrate are all listed as having no "significant nutritional value." A McCormick representative confirmed the amount in a 2-ounce bottle is not enough to register in a nutritional analysis statement. Since no more than 3 teaspoons are used in the following recipes, any possible carbohydrates found in the concentrate will be negligible.

20 ounces distilled water
6 ounces grain alcohol
1 cup Splenda
3 teaspoons Root Beer Concentrate
1 tablespoon glycerin

Add all ingredients except glycerin to a clean 32-ounce canning jar. Close lid and shake for a good 10 seconds.

Line a funnel with a conical coffee filter and pour the *LCB* Root Beer Schnapps into a decorative quart-sized bottle. Add glycerin. Shake for a few seconds.

Label and date the liqueur. Store in a dark place for at least 1 week.

One thing I've noticed when using the McCormick extracts in making a clear liqueur like Sambuca, for instance, is that the *LCB* liqueur will immediately cloud up when the extract hits the combination of grain alcohol and water. Don't panic if this happens to you. Just wait about a week or so and the liqueur will brighten. You also might see sediment on the bottom of all your *LCB* liqueurs, even months after you've filtered them. If this bothers you, filter it again, but I just pour the liqueur carefully, leaving most of the residual material on the bottom of the bottle.

Here's an example of an Amaretto made with McCormick pure extracts.

Low-Carb Bartender Amaretto II
Approximately 28 1-ounce servings:
2.53 carbohydrates per serving

For variety, we're going to use 60° as a base for this *LCB* Amaretto and "assume" that grain alcohol is actually 200° (it's really 190° or so, so we're massaging the numbers for the sake of simplicity). You can serve this immediately, but if you let it sit at least 2 weeks or more after bottling, it will allow the flavors to blend together and mellow.

19 ounces distilled water
1½ cups Splenda
¾ cup Sugar Twin brown sugar
7 ounces grain alcohol
4 ounces pure almond extract
2 teaspoons pure vanilla extract
1 tablespoon glycerin

Combine water and Splenda in a saucepan over medium heat. Heat slightly until all of the Splenda is dissolved. Remove the pan from the heat.

After 5 minutes, and while the mixture is still warm, add the Sugar Twin brown sugar. Stir until the Sugar Twin brown sugar is dissolved. Cool the mixture for another 10 minutes.

Pour the sweetened water mixture into a quart-sized canning jar. Add grain alcohol, pure almond extract, and pure vanilla extract into the sugar-free mixture. Put the lid on the jar, tighten, and shake the canning jar for a good 10 seconds. Store in a cool, dark corner for 1 week or until the *LCB* liqueur clears.

Using a funnel with a conical coffee filter inserted into it, slowly pour the *Low-Carb Bartender* Amaretto into a decorative quart-sized bottle, being careful to leave any apparent sediment behind in the canning jar. Add glycerin. Shake.

Label and date the liqueur. Store in a dark place.

Okay, now that we have an arsenal of *LCB* liqueurs in our bar, let's put together some *LCB* mixed drinks using them. Remember—be creative. Use your imagination and add some spice and variety to your *Low-Carb Bartender* drinks!

6

Mixed Drink Recipes Using
Low-Carb Bartender Liqueurs

LIQUEURS WERE PROBABLY THE END RESULT of the first attempts to disguise the harsh tastes of early distilled liquors. By combining herbs, seeds, or fruits with primitive liquors and adding honey or sugar to sweeten the harsh base of raw liquor, liqueurs took on mellower guises. In time, liqueurs even took on "medicinal" qualities as monks with too much time on their hands worked to perfect the stimulating effects of these drinks (think Benedictine).

Liqueurs are made using one or more of three methods—maceration, percolation, and distillation. Maceration refers to the practice of immersing the herbs, seeds, or fruits in a liquor base and letting their flavors and oils infuse into the liquor. The flavored base is then redistilled to capture the flavors and leave the residual material behind. This practice is somewhat the same method used in the making of homemade liqueurs, though soaking flavorings in various distilled products and then filtering the liqueur substitutes for the distillation process. Percolation is a method used to extract flavors that is analogous to the way that coffee was once made. Flavoring materials are layered in holding tanks above the liquor. The liquor is then pumped up and over the flavoring elements and allowed to seep, or percolate, back through them to the liquor below. The flavored base is then redistilled. After the flavors have been extracted using maceration or percolation and redistilled, sweeteners, and sometimes coloring, are added.

Too bad those experimenting medieval monks didn't have Splenda and essences to work with!

Acapulco
1 serving: 2 carbohydrates

A combination of a margarita and a daiquiri. The use of egg whites has fallen out of fashion but its addition makes for a frothy drink. You can omit the egg white from the drink if so desired.

1 ounce light rum
¼ ounce *LCB* Orange Brandy
1 pasteurized egg white
½ ounce lime juice
½ teaspoon Splenda

Half-fill shaker with ice. Add all ingredients. Shake well. Strain into a chilled cocktail glass.

Anisette Cocktail
1 serving: 1.4 carbohydrates

Anisette, sometimes called anise, was developed in the early twentieth century to replace the more notorious—and now banned—absinthe liqueur. Absinthe purportedly had hallucinogenic qualities.

1 ounce gin
½ ounce *LCB* Anisette
½ ounce heavy or whipping cream
1 dash nutmeg

Half-fill shaker with ice. Pour in gin, *LCB* Anisette, and cream. Shake.

Strain into a cocktail glass. Dash of nutmeg on top.

Between the Sheets
1 serving: 1.25 carbohydrates

A couple of these and you'll probably understand where the name for this drink came from.

1 ounce white brandy
½ ounce white rum
½ ounce *LCB* Orange Brandy
1 teaspoon lemon juice

Half-fill shaker with ice. Add all ingredients. Shake well. Strain into a chilled cocktail glass.

Black Russian
1 serving: 1.35 carbohydrates

If you add 1 ounce of whipping or heavy cream to the drink, it becomes a White Russian.

1 ounce vodka
½ ounce *LCB* Mexican Coffee Liqueur

Pour all ingredients into an old-fashioned glass. Stir. Add ice.

Boscoe
1 serving: 2.85 carbohydrates

Use any amber-colored tequila labeled as *reposado* to bring out the chocolate and coffee tastes of the *LCB* liqueur.

1 ounce tequila
½ ounce *LCB* Mexican Coffee Liqueur
4 ounces heavy or whipping cream

In a cocktail glass, pour in tequila and *LCB* Mexican Coffee Liqueur. Add ice. Top off with cream. Stir.

Bourble

1 serving: 1.4 carbohydrates

If you don't have bourbon on hand, you can use whiskey in this recipe.

1 ounce bourbon
½ ounce *LCB* Triple Sec or Orange Brandy
½ ounce lemon juice

Fill shaker with all ingredients and ice. Shake well. Pour into a cocktail glass.

Brave Bull

1 serving: 1.5 carbohydrates

Originally a combination of two south-of-the-border products, tequila and Kahlúa, this *LCB* version will fool everyone with its great taste.

1 ounce tequila
½ ounce *LCB* Mexican Coffee Liqueur
1 lime wedge

In a cocktail glass, pour in tequila and *LCB* Mexican Coffee Liqueur. Add ice. Stir. Garnish with lime wedge.

Easy Going

1 serving: < 1 carbohydrate

The addition of *LCB* Orange Brandy to this drink will make even the cheapest vodka "easy going" down.

1 ounce vodka
½ ounce *LCB* Orange Brandy

Add vodka and *LCB* Orange Brandy into an old-fashioned glass. Add ice. Stir.

Fancy Bourbon

1 serving: 1.9 carbohydrates

The sweet—but low-carb—addition of Splenda and *LCB* Orange Brandy fancies up this drink.

1 ounce bourbon
½ teaspoon *LCB* Orange Brandy
½ teaspoon Splenda
2 dashes Angostura bitters
1 lemon twist

Half-fill shaker with ice. Add all ingredients except lemon twist. Shake well. Strain into a cocktail glass. Garnish with lemon twist.

Fancy Brandy

I serving: < I carbohydrate

Another sweet "fancy" drink that substitutes brandy for bourbon.

1 ounce dark brandy
½ teaspoon *LCB* Orange Brandy
2 dashes Angostura bitters
1 lemon twist

Half-fill shaker with ice. Add all ingredients except lemon twist. Shake well. Strain into a cocktail glass. Garnish with lemon twist.

Itchy Bitchy

I serving: < I carbohydrate

If you don't have a clear white brandy on hand, a darker version will also work here.

¾ ounce vodka
¾ ounce white brandy
¼ ounce *LCB* Orange Brandy

Pour all ingredients into an old-fashioned glass. Stir. Add ice.

La Dolce Prima
1 serving: 3.8 carbohydrates

Be careful with this drink. It's so darn tasty that you might get carried away. Remember—moderation is the key to any weight-loss program.

1 ounce *LCB* Amaretto
1 ounce heavy or whipping cream

Half-fill shaker with ice. Pour in *LCB* Amaretto and cream. Shake. Strain into a cocktail glass.

Margarita
1 serving: 2.5 carbohydrates

Though mixed preparations like Baja Bob's Margarita Mixes can do the trick when making margaritas, the homemade version with its inclusion of fresh lime juice is a real taste delight.

1 ounce tequila
¾ ounce lime juice
½ ounce *LCB* Orange Brandy
1 lime wedge

Half-fill shaker with ice. Add all ingredients except lime wedge. Shake well.

Rub lime wedge around rim of cocktail or coupette glass. Swirl the wet rim in salt. Strain drink into glass. Garnish with lime wedge.

Mexacola

1 serving: 1.55 carbohydrates

The call for an elegant snifter glass suggests the use of a quality aged *anejo* tequila in this drink.

½ ounce tequila
½ ounce *LCB* Mexican Coffee Liqueur
1 dash cinnamon

Pour ingredients into a snifter glass. Swirl. Sprinkle cinnamon on top.

XYZ Cocktail

1 serving: 1.05 carbohydrates

Triple Sec is normally added to this drink but the *LCB* Orange Brandy is versatile enough as an excellent low-carb substitution.

1 ounce dark rum
½ ounce *LCB* Orange Brandy
1 tablespoon lemon juice

Half-fill shaker with ice. Add all ingredients. Shake well. Strain into a chilled cocktail glass.

7

Carbohydrate Counts of Popular Wines, Champagnes, Sparkling Wines, and Wine Blends

MY EFFORTS IN TRYING TO FIND the carbohydrate counts of wines were sometimes more fruitless (no pun intended) than my earlier efforts to find the carbohydrate counts of beer. Wine makers as a whole know little about what's in their wines except residual sugar content and alcoholic strength. I held my tongue whenever vintners tried to cloud the issue of what was in their wine—especially after admitting that they didn't know the carbohydrate contents of their products—by assuring me that "There is no fat in our wine." Duh! I was waiting to hear them add "never had it—never will."

From another winemaker who must have fallen asleep in Winemaking 101: "All our wines are fermented completely dry. All sugar has been fermented to alcohol." Of course, no substance can achieve 100% fermentability. Even fermented and then distilled products won't hit an absolute purity in alcohol. I won't mention the name of the company or the representative who made this comment, but this has to be one of the more absurd comments that came back to me when I researched this section of the book.

The most bizarre response from a winemaker—who also claimed to be a doctor—followed the same "logic" that dry wine ferments out with no residual sugar and therefore has no carbohydrate content. I like to refer to the following explanation from the good doctor as the "negative calorie effect."

> *Research has also discovered that the apparent calories of wine are "empty" because of the unusual situation in that the energy needed for the body to burn the calories in wine is essentially the same as the measured calories or carbohydrate count in the wine—making it a "wash."*

Thank you, doctor, but I suggest that readers "wash" the idea from their minds that certain foods or drinks can somehow negate the caloric values of themselves—including wine.

Many vintners I contacted, however, applauded my efforts to bring the idea of moderate wine drinking to LC dieters but couldn't help with carb counts. Some, quite frankly, simply didn't care. Exceptions were the fine people at E. & J. Gallo Winery and Diageo & Estates Wines Company. The depths of their wine portfolios are astonishing—their knowledge of what's in their wines was even more so. As a result of their cooperation in bringing you most of this section of wines with their carb counts, I highly recommend the Gallo and Diageo families of products for any *Low-Carb Bartender* dieter who enjoys the fermented squeezings of "the noble grape."

Although some might quibble, I've used a 5-ounce serving as the standard pour for wine. Along with recommendations by some public advocacy groups for the TTB to mandate the listing of nutritional analyses and ingredients on the labels of all alcohol-based beverages, is the further request to establish what a serving size actually is, be it wine, beer, or spirits. In April of 2004, the TTB made a tentative ruling that 5 ounces constitutes a serving of wine. In some cases, there are exceptions to my standardization of a 5-ounce wine serving in the wine/carb list, as seen with vermouths (1 ounce per serving) and wine blends (up to 8 ounces per serving).

Since the making of wine seems to elicit the same sort of confusion that beer does, the following is a brief overview of the winemaking process with an emphasis on why there are carbohydrates in wine:

Wine is actually simpler in its production than beer. Grapes are de-stemmed and then crushed to release the sugar-filled juices. If a white wine is desired, the skins of white grapes are separated from the juice. If making a red wine, the skins of red grapes are allowed to sit with the grape juice during the initial stages of fermentation. A rosé, or blush wine, spends less time in contact with the grape skins and therefore picks up only a hint of red.

When the desired effect is achieved in color and acidity, the skins are removed and cultured yeast is added to the juice to begin fermentation. Depending on the residual sugar profile the vintner desires, the fermentation is stopped accordingly. A filtering agent is added to the young wine to drop any sediment and yeast to the bottom of the holding tank. How long or short a time a wine is allowed to ferment is what will determine the residual sugar content and the resultant carbohydrates in the wine. In some cases, however, winemakers will also add grape juice to bring up the sweetness level if they've missed their target.

Wines are usually aged in stainless steel tanks, oak barrels, or a combination of the two. This depends on the type of wine and flavor desired. Before bottling, tartaric acid can be added to wine to stabilize it and to sometimes offset and counterbalance a wine with excessive sugar levels. Sulfites are also added to most wines to stop any chance of a secondary fermentation in the bottle and must be listed on the wine's label if the sulfite level exceeds ten or more parts per million, measured as total sulphur dioxide. On average, white wines seem to display the highest sulfite levels.

The claim that wines have antioxidants in them that may block free radicals, prevent heart disease, cancer, and other conditions associated with aging seems to have some validity. Polyphenol, catechin, and cholesterol-reducing resveratrol are found predominately in red wines in various degrees. One suggestion as to why some of these antioxidants are present in red wines is that grapes that have been distressed during their growth will exhibit the highest level of antioxidants. Red-skinned grapes seem to have better growing success in less temperate climates but exhibit the effects of stressful weather conditions in the form of higher levels of resveratrol. Before all you wine enthusiasts start shouting, "I told you so!" let me point out that many of the same antioxidant benefits can also be found in dark beers, too.

What we're most concerned about with wine, however, is its carbohydrate count, loosely a function of the residual sugar content. Although residual sugar levels are often made available by vintners and are a good indication as to the possible dryness or sweetness of a wine (the higher the number, the sweeter the wine), we can't, unfortunately, extrapolate the carbohydrate count of the wine from this figure without a full lab analysis.

What kind of a margin of error does the Alcohol and Tobacco Tax and Trade Bureau allow in the measurement of carbohydrates in wine? From the ATF/TTB ruling:

> *Statements of carbohydrates and fat contents are acceptable provided the actual carbohydrate or fat contents, as determined by ATF lab analysis, are within a reasonable range below, but in no case more than 20% above, the labeled amount.*

For any wine with an alcohol content of less than 7% by volume, the Food and Drug Administration actually has jurisdiction over the nutritional labeling of the product. However, the TTB has jurisdiction over the mandated government warnings that are also found on the labels of these wines and of all alcohol-based products. This is one of the few times that the FDA gets involved in the realm of spirited beverages with the TTB. You'll also find nutritional information on ciders under 7%. You should also note that some "wine" products listed here are actually derived from malt—not grapes—but have taken on the guise of a wine blend.

Almaden

Blush Chablis	5 oz	7 g
Cabernet Sauvignon	5 oz	4.7 g
Chardonnay	5 oz	5 g
Chenin Blanc	5 oz	6.1 g
Golden Chablis	5 oz	6.7 g
Light Chablis	5 oz	6 g
Light White Zinfandel	5 oz	8 g
Mellow Burgundy	5 oz	5 g
Merlot	5 oz	4.7 g
Mountain Burgundy	5 oz	5.7 g
Mountain Chablis	5 oz	4.2 g
Mountain Rhine	5 oz	8.4 g
Mountain Rosé	5 oz	8.4 g
Red Sangria	5 oz	11.8 g
White Grenache	5 oz	6.8 g
White Sangria	5 oz	10.8 g
White Zinfandel	5 oz	8.3 g

Anapamu

Chardonnay (Monterey County '01)	5 oz	3.6 g
Pinot Noir (Monterey County '01)	5 oz	3.75 g
Riesling (Monterey County '01)	5 oz	5 g
Syrah (Paso Robles '01)	5 oz	4 g

André

Andre Blush (Pink)	5 oz	9.5 g
Andre Brut	5 oz	6.5 g
Andre Cold Duck	5 oz	11 g
Andre Extra Dry	5 oz	9.5 g
Andre Mimosa Royale	5 oz	16 g
Andre Spumante	5 oz	14 g

Badger Mountain

Organic Merlot ('00)	5 oz	2.4 g

Ballatore

Ballatore Rosso	5 oz	15.5 g
Ballatore Gran Sumante	5 oz	15.5 g

Bartles & Jaymes (Malt-Based)

Black Cherry	12 oz	32 g
Classic Original	12 oz	29 g
Exotic Berry	12 oz	33 g
Fuzzy Navel	12 oz	39 g
Hard Lemonade	12 oz	39 g
Juicy Peach	12 oz	33 g
Kiwi Strawberry	12 oz	39 g
Luscious Blackberry	12 oz	39 g
Margarita	12 oz	46 g
Pina Colada	12 oz	48 g
Raspberry Daiquiri	12 oz	36 g
Raspberry Hard Lemonade	12 oz	39 g
Strawberry Cosmopolitan	12 oz	37 g
Strawberry Daiquiri	12 oz	36 g
Tropical Burst	12 oz	37 g

Barton & Guestier

Cabernet Sauvignon ('02)	5 oz	1.7 g
Chardonnay ('02)	5 oz	1.1 g
French Tom Cabernet Sauvignon ('02)	5 oz	1.3 g
French Tom Chardonnay ('02)	5 oz	1.1 g
French Tom Merlot ('01)	5 oz	1.4 g
Merlot ('02)	5 oz	1.6 g

Barton & Guestier (continued)

Sauvignon Blanc ('03)	5 oz	.9 g
Shiraz('02)	5 oz	1.2 g

Beaulieu Vineyard (BV)

California Syrah ('00)	5 oz	1.7 g
Century Cellars Chardonnay ('02)	5 oz	1.7 g
Century Cellars Merlot ('01)	5 oz	1.8 g
Century Cellars Sauvignon Blanc ('02)	5 oz	1.5 g
Coastal Estates Cabernet Sauvignon ('01)	5 oz	1.4 g
Coastal Estates Chardonnay ('02)	5 oz	1.9 g
Coastal Estates Merlot ('01)	5 oz	1.4 g
Coastal Estates Pinot Noir ('01)	5 oz	1.5 g
Coastal Estates Sauvignon Blanc ('02)	5 oz	1.1 g
Coastal Estates Shiraz ('02)	5 oz	1.5 g
Coastal Estates Zinfandel ('02)	5 oz	1.5 g
Dulcet ('00)	5 oz	1.6 g
Georges de Latour Reserve		
Cabernet Sauvignon Blanc ('03)	5 oz	1.7 g
Napa Valley Cabernet Sauvignon ('00)	5 oz	1.8 g
Napa Valley Merlot ('01)	5 oz	1.6 g
Napa Valley Sauvignon Blanc ('01)	5 oz	1.4 g
Napa Valley Zinfandel ('01)	5 oz	1.5 g
Reserve Chardonnay ('00)	5 oz	1.8 g
Reserve Pinot Noir ('00)	5 oz	1.5 g
Signet Cabernet Sauvignon ('01)	5 oz	1.5 g
Signet Chardonnay ('01)	5 oz	1.8 g
Signet Merlot ('01)	5 oz	1.7 g
Tapestry ('00)	5 oz	1.6 g

Bella Sera

Cabernet Sauvignon ('98)	5 oz	4.55 g
Cabernet Sauvignon ('01)	5 oz	3.9 g
Chardonnay Delle Venezie ('00)	5 oz	3.6 g
Merlot ('98)	5 oz	4.4 g
Merlot ('00)	5 oz	4.25 g
Merlot ('01)	5 oz	3.95 g
Pinot Grigio ('99)	5 oz	3.95 g
Pinot Grigio ('00)	5 oz	3.1 g
Pinot Grigio ('02)	5 oz	3.15 g
Sangiovese ('98)	5 oz	4.15 g
Sangiovese ('00)	5 oz	4.35 g
Sangiovese ('01)	5 oz	3.9 g

Black Swan

Chardonnay ('02)	5 oz	4 g
Shiraz ('02)	5 oz	5.15 g
Cabernet Sauvignon ('02)	5 oz	4.9 g
Merlot ('02)	5 oz	4.8 g

Boone's Farm

Blackberry (Malt)	5 oz	16.5 g
Blackberry (Apple)	5 oz	16.5 g
Country Kwencher (Apple)	5 oz	12.5 g
Fuzzy Navel (Malt)	5 oz	24.5 g
Fuzzy Navel (Apple)	5 oz	18.5 g
Hard Lemonade (Malt)	5 oz	16.5 g
Hard Lemonade (Apple)	5 oz	15.5 g
Kiwi Strawberry (Citrus)	5 oz	13.5 g
Mountain Berry (Malt)	5 oz	14.5 g
Pina Colada (Malt)	5 oz	19.5 g
Raspberry Hard Lemonade (Malt)	5 oz	16 g

Boone's Farm (continued)

Raspberry Hard Lemonade (Apple)	5 oz	15.5 g
Sangria (Grape)	5 oz	14 g
Snow Creek Berry (Apple)	5 oz	14.5 g
Strawberry Daiquiri (Malt)	5 oz	15.5 g
Strawberry Daiquiri (Apple)	5 oz	16.5 g
Strawberry Hill (Grape)	5 oz	14.5 g
Strawberry Hill (Citrus)	5 oz	14 g
Sun Peak Peach (Malt)	5 oz	14 g
Sun Peak Peach (Apple)	5 oz	14.5 g
Wild Island (Apple)	5 oz	16.5 g

Cantine Aurora Tortona

Piemonte Frizzante ('01)	5 oz	21.5 g

Cantine Riunite

White Lambrusco	5 oz	8.1 g
Strawberry White Merlot	5 oz	11.58 g
Spumante	5 oz	9.23 g
Raspberry Cabernet	5 oz	11.58 g
Rosato	5 oz	8.93 g
Raspberry	5 oz	12.5 g
Peach Chardonnay	5 oz	11.58 g
Peach	5 oz	11.01 g
Lambrusco	5 oz	8.9 g
D'Oro	5 oz	9.38 g
Blackberry Merlot	5 oz	11.58 g
Cabernet	5 oz	11.58 g
Bianco	5 oz	8.9 g

Carlo Rossi

Blush	5 oz	7.5 g
Burgundy	5 oz	5.5 g
Chablis	5 oz	5 g
Cabernet Sauvignon	5 oz	5 g
Chianti	5 oz	5.5 g
Paisano	5 oz	6.5 g
Rhine	5 oz	8 g
Sangria (Spanada)	5 oz	11.5 g
Vin Rosé	5 oz	7.5 g
White Grenache	5 oz	7 g
White Zinfandel	5 oz	7.5 g

Chateau Haut-Brion

Haut-Brion ('99)	4 oz	1.75 g

Chateau Latour

Grand Vin de Chateau Latour ('99)	5 oz	2.2 g

Dominus Estate

Napa Valley ('99)	5 oz	2.41 g

Ecco Domani

Cabernet Sauvignon ('01)	5 oz	4 g
Chianti ('01)	5 oz	3.6 g
Merlot ('01)	5 oz	4.05 g
Pinot Bianco ('96)	5 oz	3.5 g
Pinot Grigio ('02)	5 oz	3.15 g
Pinot Nero ('96)	5 oz	4 g
Sangiovese ('96)	5 oz	4 g
Sangiovese ('01)	5 oz	4 g

Eden Roc

Brut	5 oz	5 g
Brut Rosé	5 oz	10 g
Extra Dry	5 oz	5 g

E. & J. Gallo Winery

Vermouth Extra Dry	1 oz	.8 g
Vermouth Sweet	1 oz	4.4 g

Ernest & Julio Gallo (Twin Valley)

Cabernet Sauvignon	5 oz	3.5 g
Café Chardonnay	5 oz	8 g
Café Zinfandel	5 oz	6 g
Chardonnay	5 oz	4.5 g
Hearty Burgundy	5 oz	4.5 g
Merlot	5 oz	3.5 g
Sauvignon Blanc	5 oz	4.5 g
Shiraz	5 oz	5.25 g
White Merlot	5 oz	4.5 g
White Zinfandel	5 oz	3.5 g

Errazuriz

Don Maximiano ('99)	5 oz	3.01 g

Fairbanks

Cream Sherry	5 oz	20 g
Port	5 oz	20 g
Sherry	5 oz	10 g
White Port	5 oz	20 g

Fre (Sutter Home) Non Alcoholic

White Zinfandel	5 oz	11.88 g
Chardonnay	5 oz	10.63 g
Sparkling Brut	5 oz	10 g
Spumante	5 oz	16.88 g
Merlot	5 oz	11.88 g
Premium Red	5 oz	12.5 g
Premium White	5 oz	11.88 g

Frei Brothers (Redwood Creek)

Cabernet Sauvignon ('99)	5 oz	3.75 g
Cabernet Sauvignon ('00)	5 oz	4.45 g
Chardonnay ('00)	5 oz	4.25 g
Chardonnay ('01)	5 oz	3.8 g
Merlot ('00)	5 oz	4.95 g
Merlot ('01)	5 oz	4.85 g
Syrah ('01)	5 oz	5.2 g
Pinot Grigio ('02)	5 oz	3.25 g
Sauvignon Blanc ('00)	5 oz	3.8 g
Sauvignon Blanc ('01)	5 oz	3.5 g

Frey

Zinfandel ('01)	5 oz	2.01 g

Gallo Sonoma

Cabernet Sauvignon (Sonoma County '96)	5 oz	4.5 g
Cabernet Sauvignon (Sonoma County '97)	5 oz	4.5 g
Cabernet Sauvignon (Sonoma County '98)	5 oz	4.5 g
Cabernet Sauvignon (Sonoma County '99)	5 oz	4.5 g
Chardonnay (Russian River Valley '97)	5 oz	4.5 g
Chardonnay (Russian River Valley '98)	5 oz	4 g
Chardonnay (Sonoma County '99)	5 oz	4 g

Gallo Sonoma (continued)

Chardonnay (Sonoma County '00)	5 oz	4.5 g
Merlot (Sonoma County '97)	5 oz	4 g
Merlot (Sonoma County '98)	5 oz	4.5 g
Merlot (Sonoma County '99)	5 oz	4.5 g
Pinot Gris (Sonoma County '00)	5 oz	4.5 g
Pinot Noir (Russian River Valley '97)	5 oz	4 g
Pinot Noir (Russian River Valley '98)	5 oz	4 g
Pinot Noir (Sonoma County '99)	5 oz	4.5 g
Sangiovese (Alexander Valley '97)	5 oz	4 g
Sangiovese (Alexander Valley '98)	5 oz	4.5 g
Sangiovese (Sonoma County '99)	5 oz	5 g
Zinfandel (Sonoma County '96)	5 oz	4.5 g
Zinfandel (Sonoma County '96)	5 oz	5 g
Zinfandel (Dry Creek Valley '98)	5 oz	4.5 g

Gossamer Bay

Cabernet Sauvignon ('01)	5 oz	5.5 g
Chardonnay ('01)	5 oz	5.5 g
Merlot ('01)	5 oz	4.5 g
Pinot Grigio ('01)	5 oz	7.5 g
White Zinfandel	5 oz	7.5 g

Indigo Hills

Brut Chardonnay Champagne	5 oz	4 g
Blanc de Blanc	5 oz	4.55 g
Cabernet Sauvignon (North Coast '00)	5 oz	3.75 g
Carbernet Sauvignon (California '00)	5 oz	3.6 g
Chardonnay (Central Coast '00)	5 oz	3.55 g
Chardonnay (Central Coast '01)	5 oz	3.75 g
Merlot (San Francisco Bay Livermore '00)	5 oz	5.3 g
Merlot (California '01)	5 oz	3.7 g
Pinot Noir (North Coast '01)	5 oz	3.4 g

Livingston Cellars

Blush Chablis	5 oz	7.5 g
Burgundy	5 oz	4.5 g
Cabernet Sauvignon	5 oz	5.5 g
Chablis Blanc	5 oz	5 g
Chardonnay (Italy)	5 oz	5 g
Chianti	5 oz	5.5 g
French Colombard	5 oz	5.5 g
Merlot	5 oz	4.5 g
Red Rosé	5 oz	10 g
Rhine	5 oz	8 g
White Zinfandel	5 oz	7.5 g

Marcelina

Cabernet Sauvignon Napa ('93)	5 oz	4.1 g
Chardonnay Napa ('00)	5 oz	3.55 g
Chardonnay Carneros ('01)	5 oz	2.8 g
Pinot Noir Carneros ('00)	5 oz	3.9 g
Merlot Napa ('00)	5 oz	5.05 g

McWilliam's Wines

Chardonnay ('02)	5 oz	3.4 g
Cabernet Sauvignon ('02)	5 oz	4.8 g
Merlot ('02)	5 oz	4.75 g
Shiraz ('02)	5 oz	6.15 g

Niebaum Coppola

Rubicon ('99)	5 oz	2.6 g

Peter Vella

Blush	5 oz	7.5 g
Burgundy	5 oz	5 g

Peter Vella (continued)

Cabernet Sauvignon	5 oz	5.5 g
Chablis	5 oz	6 g
Chardonnay	5 oz	6 g
Delicious Red	5 oz	7 g
Merlot	5 oz	5 g
White Grenache	5 oz	7 g
White Zinfandel	5 oz	8.5 g

Rancho Zabaco

Cabernet Port	5 oz	19.5 g
Chardonnay (Russian River Valley '99)	5 oz	4.5 g
Pinot Gris (Sonoma Coast '01)	5 oz	3.45 g
Pinot Gris (Sonoma Coast '02)	5 oz	2.15 g
Sauvignon Blanc (Russian River Valley '01)	5 oz	3 g
Sauvignon (Russian River Valley '02)	5 oz	2.7 g
Syrah (Sonoma Coast '00)	5 oz	5.35 g
Zinfandel (Dry Creek Valley '00)	5 oz	5.55 g
Zinfandel (Dry Creek Valley '01)	5 oz	4.3 g
Zinfandel (Sonoma Heritage Vines '00)	5 oz	5.2 g
Zinfandel (Sonoma Heritage Vines '01)	5 oz	4.45 g
Zinfandel (Chioti '00)	5 oz	4.05 g
Zinfandel (Chioti '01)	5 oz	4.05 g
Zinfandel (Stefani '99)	5 oz	3.9 g
Zinfandel (Stefani '01)	5 oz	3.75 g

Sheffield Cellars

Sherry	5 oz	20 g
Tawny Port	5 oz	20 g
Vermouth Dry	1 oz	1 g
Vermouth Extra Dry	1 oz	1 g
Vermouth Sweet	1 oz	4 g

Very Dry Sherry	5 oz	5 g
Madeira	5 oz	14.29 g
Port	5 oz	15.71 g
Red	5 oz	2.86 g
Rose	5 oz	2.86 g
Sherry	5 oz	12.5 g
Sweet Dessert	5 oz	17.5 g

Sterling Vineyards

3 Palms Merlot ('00)	5 oz	1.8 g
Diamond Mountain Ranch Cabernet Sauvignon ('00)	5 oz	1.8 g
Diamond Mountain Ranch Merlot ('00)	5 oz	1.5 g
Napa Valley Cabernet Sauvignon ('00)	5 oz	1.7 g
Napa Valley Chardonnay ('02)	5 oz	1.8 g
Napa Valley Merlot ('00)	5 oz	1.6 g
Napa Valley Sauvgnon Blanc ('02)	5 oz	1.6 g
Reserve Cabernet Sauvignon ('00)	5 oz	1.8 g
Reserve Chardonnay ('00)	5 oz	1.6 g
Reserve Merlot ('00)	5 oz	1.7 g
Vintner's Collection Cabernet Sauvignon ('01)	5 oz	2.1 g
Vintner's Collection Chardonnay ('02)	5 oz	1.7 g
Vintner's Collection Merlot ('01)	5 oz	2.2 g
Vintner's Collection Pinot Noir ('02)	5 oz	1.3 g
Vintner's Collection Shiraz ('02)	5 oz	2.1 g
Winery Lake Chardonnay ('01)	5 oz	1.9 g
Winery Lake Merlot ('00)	5 oz	1.6 g
Winery Lake Pinot Noir ('01)	5 oz	1.7 g

Sutter Home

Cabernet Sauvignon	5 oz	3.38 g
Chardonnay	5 oz	3.88 g

Sutter Home (continued)

Chenin Blanc	5 oz	7.75 g
Gewurztraminer	5 oz	7 g
Merlot	5 oz	3.88 g
Moscato	5 oz	14 g
Pinot Noir	5 oz	3.13 g
Sauvignon Blanc	5 oz	2.88 g
Shiraz	5 oz	3.38 g
White Zinfandel	5 oz	5.88 g
Zinfandel	5 oz	3.38 g

Thunderbird

Nighttrain	5 oz	15.5 g
Thunderbird (Red Label 17.5%)	5 oz	15.5 g
Thunderbird (Blue Label 13.5%)	5 oz	15 g

Tott's

Tott's Blanc de Noir	5 oz	10 g
Tott's Brut	5 oz	5 g
Tott's Extra Dry	5 oz	7 g

Turning Leaf

Cabernet Sauvignon (San Luis Obispo '96)	5 oz	5 g
Cabernet Sauvignon (Coastal '97)	5 oz	5.5 g
Chardonnay (Sonoma County '98)	5 oz	4 g
Chardonnay (North Coast '98)	5 oz	4 g
Chardonnay (North Coast '99)	5 oz	4 g
Merlot (Sonoma County '97)	5 oz	4.5 g
Merlot (Coastal '98)	5 oz	4.5 g
Merlot (Coastal '99)	5 oz	4.5 g
Pinot Noir (North Coast '98)	5 oz	4.5 g
Pinot Noir (North Coast '99)	5 oz	4.5 g

Zinfandel ('96)	5 oz.	4.5 g
Zinfandel ('98)	5 oz	5 g
Zinfandel ('99)	5 oz	5 g

Wine Blends

Arbor Mist

Tropical Fruits Chardonnay	8 oz	21 g
Strawberry White Zinfandel	8 oz	20 g
Blackberry Merlot	8 oz	21 g
Sangria Zinfandel	8 oz	18 g
Exotic Fruits White Zinfandel	8 oz	22 g
Cranberry Twist White Merlot	8 oz	21 g
Peach Chardonnay	8 oz	17 g
Melon White Zinfandel	8 oz	19 g

Boone's Farm (Flavored Apple Wines)

Strawberry Daiquiri	8 oz	25 g
Wild Island	8 oz	26 g
Melon Ball	8 oz	26 g
Snow Creek Berry	8 oz	23 g
Blackberry Ridge	8 oz	27 g
Hard Lemonade	8 oz	26 g
Wild Raspberry	8 oz	25 g
Raspberry Hard Lemonade	8 oz	25 g

8

Wine-, Champagne-, and Sparkling Wine-Based Drinks

I KNOW, SOME OF YOU ARE ALREADY SAYING, "Why ruin a good wine or champagne by making it into a mixed drink?" Once again, though, I remind you that *The Low-Carb Bartender* is not about boring predictability—the same old thing, the same old food, the same old drinks. Boredom is the death of a LC diet. This chapter is an attempt to help you look beyond the snob appeal that sometimes lingers over wine appreciation. But please, forget about pulling out a reserve bottling to make a "wine spritzer" or dusting off a magnum of Dom Perignon for the ubiquitous "champagne cocktail." Take a chance with a cheaper brand of wine or a sparkling wine and have a little fun while you still keep those carbs on track!

There is a distinction between champagne and sparkling wines. Champagne undergoes a secondary fermentation in the bottle, known as *méthode champenoise*, that puts the bubbles in the product. The secondary fermentation occurs because of the addition of yeast nutrients and sugar. Sparkling wines also get their bubbles from an addition of yeast nutrients and sugar, but this bulk processing, or *charmat* process, of adding carbon dioxide to the wine is done in a huge pressurized stainless steel tank rather than in individual bottles. It's said that one way to tell true champagne from a sparkling wine is by the size of the bubbles—the smaller, the better.

How can you tell a "dry" champagne or sparkling wine from a sweeter version? Check the label. In order of dryness, *Natural* or *Brut Nature* is very dry; *Brut* is dry; *Extra Dry* is slightly sweet (an oxymoron, for sure); *Sec*, *Demi-Sec*, and *Doux* are considered sweet, with the last being the sweetest. For you LC dieters who like to split hairs about whether red wines are more beneficial than white or vice versa, *Blanc de Blanc* on champagne or sparkling wine labels refers to a product made from white grapes—*Blanc de Noirs*, from red grapes.

Not surprisingly, more champagne and sparkling wine is consumed per capita in Washington, D.C., than anywhere else in the United States.

To standardize these drink recipes, I've used Eden Roc Extra Dry and also the word "champagne" throughout these recipes, though Eden Roc is actually a sparkling wine. Other champagne and sparkling wine brands are also listed with carbohydrate counts in Chapter 7.

Air Mail
I serving: 6.17 carbohydrates

Gold rum is often called for in this drink. You can substitute a clear rum if you don't have a gold on hand. Remember—gold rum is usually clear rum with a bit of caramel coloring added to it.

1½ ounces rum
¾ ounce lime juice
1 teaspoon Splenda
4 ounces champagne

Half-fill shaker with ice. Add rum, lime juice, and Splenda. Shake well.

Strain into a chilled highball glass. Top with cold champagne. Stir gently.

Americana
I serving: 2.5 carbohydrates

Good old American bourbon works best in this drink.

¼ ounce bourbon
½ teaspoon Splenda
1 dash Angostura bitters
2 ounces champagne

Add all ingredients into a champagne glass. Top off with cold champagne. Stir gently.

Can Can

1 serving: 2 carbohydrates

Don't forget that you can substitute sparkling wine for champagne.

1 ounce vodka
2 ounces cold champagne
1 lemon twist

Pour vodka into a champagne glass. Top off with cold champagne. Stir gently. Garnish with lemon twist.

Champagne Cocktail

1 serving: 4.75 carbohydrates

No one will ever know that you substituted Splenda for the powdered sugar this drink normally calls for.

4 ounces champagne
1 teaspoon Splenda
1 dash Angostura bitters

Pour Splenda into a champagne flute. Soak Splenda with bitters. Top off with cold champagne.

Champagne Cocktail II

1 serving: 7 carbohydrates

Brandy adds a deeper dimension to this champagne-based drink.

6 ounces champagne
1 teaspoon Splenda
2 dashes Angostura bitters
½ ounce brandy

Pour Splenda into a champagne flute. Soak Splenda with bitters.

Pour in brandy and top off with cold champagne.

Champagne Julep

1 serving: 4.65 carbohydrates

Fresh mint is indispensable in this drink. Grow a little patch of mint in your yard and forget the ordering whims of your local grocer.

4 ounces champagne
1 ounce bourbon
1 teaspoon Splenda
2 mint leaves

In a separate mixing glass, muddle the mint leaves with the Splenda and a few drops of water.

Add bourbon. Stir well and strain mixture into a collins glass half-filled with ice cubes. Top off with champagne.

Diet V8 Splash Fizz
1 serving: 5.5 carbohydrates

After using Diet V8 Splash and *LCB* Orange Brandy in this mimosa-like drink, you'll never go back to orange juice.

4 ounces champagne
½ ounce *LCB* Orange Brandy
1 ounce Diet V8 Splash, any flavor
1 orange slice

Pour champagne, *LCB* Orange Brandy, and Diet V8 Splash into a champagne flute. Garnish with orange slice.

Diet V8 Splash Mimosa
1 serving: 4.13 carbohydrates

A perfect *Low-Carb Bartender* alternative during brunch.

3 ounces Diet V8 Splash, any flavor
3 ounces champagne

Pour Diet V8 Splash into a tall flute glass. Top off with cold champagne.

Fluffy Ruffles

1 serving: 6 carbohydrates

A Prohibition-era drink invented for women who dared to be seen drinking in public. You go, girl!

1 ounces rum (dark or clear)
1½ ounces sweet vermouth
1 lemon twist

Half-fill shaker with ice. Pour in rum and sweet vermouth. Shake. Strain into a cocktail glass. Add lemon twist.

Queen's Cousin

1 serving: 5.25 carbohydrates

LCB Orange Brandy comes to the rescue again, pushing aside the Grand Marnier and Cointreau normally called for in this drink.

1 ounce vodka
1 ounce *LCB* Orange Brandy
½ ounce lime juice
2 dashes Angostura bitters
3 ounces champagne

Half-fill shaker with ice. Add vodka, *LCB* Orange Brandy, lime juice, and bitters. Shake well.

Strain into a large wine glass and top off with cold champagne. Stir gently.

Red Wine Spritzer
1 serving: 3.2 carbohydrates

This is a great drink to enjoy during a party when a glass in your hand seems almost mandatory. Low in both carbs and alcohol.

4 ounces red wine
4 ounces seltzer or soda water
1 lemon or lime twist

Half-fill highball glass with ice. Pour in red wine and seltzer or soda water. Garnish with lemon or lime twist.

Turkish Harem Cooler
1 serving: 3.2 carbohydrates

And you always thought that gin was the only thing that went with diet tonic!

4 ounces Rosé wine
4 ounces diet tonic water

Half-fill a highball glass with ice. Pour in Rosé wine and diet tonic water. Stir.

White Cobbler

1 serving: 3.5 carbohydrates

The clear, albeit sweeter, alternative to a Red Wine Spritzer.

4 ounces white wine
4 ounces seltzer or soda water
½ teaspoon Splenda

Half-fill a highball glass with ice. Pour in white wine, Splenda, and seltzer or soda water. Stir gently.

White Flame

1 serving: 6 carbohydrates

A deceptively strong, but tasty drink. Moderation, please.

1½ ounces gin
¾ ounce *LCB* Orange Brandy
4 ounces champagne

Pour gin and *LCB* Orange Brandy into a highball glass. Add ice. Top off with champagne.

White Wine Spritzer

1 serving: 3.2 carbohydrates

The white "yin" complements the "yang" of a Red Wine Spritzer. During the summer, a light pinot grigio works wonders in this drink.

4 ounces white wine
4 ounces seltzer or soda water
1 lemon or lime twist

Half-fill highball glass with ice. Pour in white wine and seltzer or soda water. Garnish with lemon or lime twist.

9

Bourbon-Based Drinks

BOURBON IS ACTUALLY A WHISKEY, probably America's first real whiskey. The grain bill consists of a mandated minimum of 51% corn, the rest of the grains being a mixture of rye and barley. The grains are mashed, and the sweet runnings fermented and then distilled. The bourbon is then aged in charred virgin oak barrels, never to be used again in the bourbon aging process. Most of these used barrels are sold to Scotch distillers and reused to age their products.

Though bourbon purists insist that bourbon, especially 100° proof, bottled-in-bond variety, is best sipped straight, these mixed bourbon drinks would probably put a smile on the face of any old Kentucky colonel, whether they were watching their carbs or not!

No bourbon? Use whiskey instead.

0 carbohydrates in bourbon.

Bourbon Cobbler
1 serving: 1.75 carbohydrates

This is a classic drink from the 1920s. Cobblers can also be mixed with virtually any distilled product. Be creative!

2 ounces bourbon
½ ounce lemon juice
1 teaspoon Splenda
4 ounces seltzer or soda water

Fill a shaker with bourbon, lemon juice, and Splenda. Shake well. Pour into a highball glass. Add ice cubes and top off with seltzer.

Bourbon Collins
1 serving: 2.5 carbohydrates

Mixed drinks called "collins" are actually generic bases that, most often, simply switch the type of liquor used. Substitute any liquor for this bourbon-inspired collins recipe and add to your *LCB* arsenal.

1½ ounces bourbon
1 ounce lemon juice
½ teaspoon Splenda
1 dash Angostura bitters
5 ounces seltzer or soda water
1 lemon wedge

Half-fill shaker with ice. Pour in bourbon, lemon juice, Splenda, and bitters. Shake.

Strain into a collins glass filled with ice. Top off with seltzer or soda water. Garnish with lemon wedge.

Bourbon Cooler
I serving: I carbohydrate

Like any collins-type drink, coolers can also be the base for any liquor you desire. Try gin or vodka, for instance, in lieu of bourbon as this drink recipe calls for. Be creative!

2 ounces bourbon
2 dashes Angostura bitters
4 ounces diet lemon-lime soda
1 slice of lime

Combine bourbon and bitters in a collins glass. Add diet lemon-lime soda and ice to fill. Stir. Garnish with lime slice.

Bourbon Fix
I serving: 2.5 carbohydrates

Another Prohibition-era drink that can also be made with whatever spirit you have on hand.

1½ ounces bourbon
1 ounce lemon juice
1 teaspoon Splenda
1 lemon wedge

Fill a highball glass with ice. Add all ingredients except lemon wedge. Stir. Garnish with lemon wedge.

Bourbon Highball
I serving: < I carbohydrate

Another classic. Use whiskey if bourbon isn't available.

1½ ounces bourbon
4 ounces diet ginger ale

Fill highball glass with ice. Pour in bourbon. Top off with diet ginger ale. Stir.

Bourbon Lancer
I serving: 4.75 carbohydrates

The carbonation in the champagne seems to quicken the effects of the bourbon. Please—no more than two of these!

½ teaspoon Splenda
1½ ounces bourbon
1 dash Angostura bitters
4 ounces champagne
1 lemon peel spiral

Add Splenda into highball glass. Pour in bourbon and dissolve. Add ice and a dash of bitters. Fill with champagne. Stir gently. Garnish with lemon peel spiral.

Bourbon Rickey

1 serving: 2.5 carbohydrates

A rickey base can also be used with any liquor desired. Bourbon works well here—but don't hold back! Remember, be creative.

1½ ounces bourbon
1 lime wedge
6 ounces seltzer or soda water

Half-fill highball glass with ice. Pour in bourbon. Squeeze lime into glass and toss in the wedge. Top off with seltzer or soda water. Stir.

Bourbon Sour

1 serving: 3 carbohydrates

As you might have guessed, a sour drink base can also hold up to any liquor you might desire.

2 ounces bourbon
1 ounce lemon juice
1 teaspoon Splenda

Half-fill shaker with ice. Add all the ingredients. Shake well. Strain into a sour glass. Add 2 ice cubes and stir.

Bourbon Swizzle

1 serving: 3.25 carbohydrates

Another great all-purpose drink that can be matched with any spirit.

2 ounces bourbon
1 ounce lemon juice
1 teaspoon Splenda
1 dash Angostura bitters
3 ounces seltzer water

Fill shaker with bourbon, lemon juice, Splenda, and bitters. Add ice cubes. Shake well.

Almost fill a collins glass with crushed ice. Strain shaker contents into glass. Top off with seltzer water. Stir.

Dry Manhattan

1 serving: < 1 carbohydrate

Though it's not called for in this drink recipe, a generous splash of Angostura bitters is a common added ingredient.

1½ ounces bourbon
¾ ounce dry vermouth
1 olive

Add two ice cubes to an old-fashioned glass. Pour in all ingredients. Stir. Garnish with olive.

Mint Julep

1 serving: .65 carbohydrate

As American as apple pie!

2 fresh mint leaves
1 teaspoon Splenda
2 ounces bourbon
1 mint sprig

Muddle the mint leaves and Splenda on the bottom of an old-fashioned glass to release mint oils.

Add bourbon and ice cubes. Stir and add mint sprig for garnish.

Oh Henry!

1 serving: 5 carbohydrates

Notice that this drink doesn't call for ice cubes. Make sure the diet ginger ale is ice cold.

1 ounce bourbon
1 ounce Benedictine
2 ounces cold diet ginger ale

Pour all ingredients into a chilled cocktail glass. Stir.

Pendennis

1 serving: < 1 carbohydrate

Another tasty example of Splenda doing a great job as a powdered sugar substitute.

$\frac{1}{2}$ teaspoon Splenda
2 ounces bourbon
1 lemon slice

Fill an old-fashioned glass with crushed ice. Add Splenda.
Pour in bourbon. Stir well and garnish with lemon slice.

Sazerac

1 serving: 1.25 carbohydrates

Legend has it that this drink is the first American cocktail, initially
appearing around 1830 in New Orleans. For this drink, put aside
the Angostura and use Peychaud's bitters, as pharmacist Antoine
Peychaud did when he developed his unique bitters and then
dreamed up the Sazerac to accommodate his elixir. Go to
www.sazerac.com/history.html to read more about this drink.

2 ounces bourbon
$\frac{1}{2}$ teaspoon Splenda
2 dashes Peychaud's bitters
4 ounces seltzer
1 lemon twist

Mix everything except seltzer in a highball glass. Stir well.
Add ice cubes and top off with seltzer. Stir again. Garnish
with lemon twist.

Westminister
1 serving: 3.75 carbohydrates

The addition of dry and sweet vermouth adds a unique dimension to this drink.

1 ounce bourbon
¾ ounce dry vermouth
¾ ounce sweet vermouth

Add 2 ice cubes to an old-fashioned glass. Pour in all ingredients. Stir.

10

Brandy-Based Drinks

BRANDY IS ACTUALLY DISTILLED WINE, customarily aged in oak barrels. Under the term "brandy" falls cognac and French Cognac (made exclusively in Cognac, a small region in southwest France). Not all brandies, however, are of French origin. Many excellent quality brandies are coming out of California, including the E&J line from Gallo.

Younger brandies are often clear in appearance and sometimes made from fruits other than grapes. Examples are Kirschwasser (cherries), Slivovitz (plums), Grappa (grape skins, pulp, and stems), and Calvados (apples).

As a rule of thumb, clear (white) brandies—products of distillation—contain zero carbs. The aged-in-oak and there-fore darker brandies pick up a small amount of carbohy-drates through tannins in the wood during the maturation process as the volume of the brandy decreases through evaporation and the color deepens. The tradeoff is a much smoother product with an ever-so-slightly higher carb count than the clear brandies.

Stay away from fruit-flavored brandies unless you know their carbohydrate counts. Most, if not all, are dosed with flavorings and sugar. Unfortunately, none of the more popular manufacturers of these products would answer my inquiries for the carbohydrate counts of their products. When in doubt, leave it out!

Adios Amigos
1 serving: 2.19 carbohydrates

With a mixture of three different liquors and a generous dash of wine, this drink is aptly named.

1 ounce white brandy
½ ounce light rum
½ ounce gin
½ ounce dry vermouth
¾ ounce lime juice

Half-fill shaker with ice. Add all ingredients. Shake well. Strain into a chilled cocktail glass.

Brandy Alexander
1 serving: 3.55 carbohydrates

Around our house, this drink has become a Christmastime favorite. You can substitute any of the Hood dairy beverages in lieu of the heavy cream if desired.

1½ ounces dark brandy
1 tablespoon Da Vinci Gourmet Sugar Free Chocolate Syrup
1½ ounce heavy (or whipping) cream
1 dash nutmeg

Half-fill shaker with ice. Add all ingredients except nutmeg. Shake well. Strain into a chilled cocktail glass. Dust lightly with ground nutmeg.

Brandy Crusta
1 serving: 1.75 carbohydrates

If you don't have a clear (white) brandy on hand, substitute with an amber-colored one or even whiskey.

1 lemon twist
2 ounces white brandy
1 teaspoon Da Vinci Gourmet Sugar Free Cherry Syrup
½ ounce lemon juice
2 dashes Angostura bitters

Rub rim of highball glass with lemon twist and toss into glass. Half-fill shaker with ice. Add all ingredients. Shake well. Strain into glass.

Brandy Fix

1 serving: 2.6 carbohydrates

A "fix" is another versatile base that works well with any distilled product.

2 ounces white brandy
1 teaspoon Splenda
1 ounce lemon juice
2 teaspoons water
1 lemon wedge

Mix brandy, Splenda, lemon juice, and water in a highball glass. Stir well. Add ice cubes. Garnish with lemon wedge.

Brandy Sling

1 serving: 2.6 carbohydrates

Various interpretations of "slings" were first developed in the early twentieth century with a woman's taste for sweets in mind. If you like, you can add 1 tablespoon of Da Vinci Gourmet Sugar Free Cherry Syrup to sweeten up this subdued version.

1½ ounces white brandy
1 ounce lemon juice
1 teaspoon Splenda
6 ounces seltzer or soda water
1 lemon twist

Pour all ingredients except lemon twist into a highball glass half-filled with ice cubes. Stir. Garnish with lemon twist.

Brandy and Soda

1 serving: 2.4 carbohydrates

In the style of a highball, this drink also works fine with clear brandy.

1½ ounces dark brandy
5 ounces seltzer

Pour the brandy and seltzer into a highball glass half-filled with ice cubes. Stir.

Brandy Sour

1 serving: 5.4 carbohydrates

A dash of Da Vinci Gourmet Sugar Free Orange and/or Cherry Syrup will brighten up this recipe if so desired.

2 ounces dark brandy
1 ounce lemon juice
1 teaspoon Splenda

Half-fill shaker with ice. Add all ingredients. Shake well. Strain into a sour glass. Add ice cubes.

Brandy Swizzle
1 serving: 2.6 carbohydrates

Another classic drink from the Prohibition era.

2 ounces brandy
1 ounce lime juice
1 teaspoon Splenda
4 ounces seltzer or soda water
2 dashes Angostura bitters

Fill a collins glass with crushed or shaved ice. Pour in all ingredients. Stir well.

Brandy Up
1 serving: < 1 carbohydrate

Although 7 Up is the implied mix for this drink, any diet lemon-lime soda will work in this highball.

1½ ounces brandy
6 ounces diet lemon-lime soda

Half-fill a highball glass with ice. Pour in all ingredients. Stir.

Dirty Mother

1 serving: 4.22 carbohydrates

Use Hood's Carb Countdown 2% Reduced Fat Chocolate Dairy Beverage instead of heavy cream for a nice variation. Drop 2 carbs from the drink's total carb count if you do!

2 ounces dark brandy
2 ounces heavy (or whipping cream)
¼ teaspoon instant coffee

Half-fill shaker with ice. Add all ingredients. Shake well. Strain and pour into a highball glass. Add ice cubes.

Metro Cocktail

1 serving: 5.15 carbohydrates

Sometimes called a Metropolitan. Just call it delicious!

2 ounces white brandy
1 ounce sweet vermouth
1 teaspoon Splenda
1 dash Angostura bitters

Half-fill shaker with ice. Add all ingredients. Shake well. Strain into a cocktail glass.

Polar Attraction

I serving: < I carbohydrate

Although its name might imply otherwise, this drink makes a
great summertime refreshment.

2 ounces white brandy
2 ounces diet tonic water
1 lemon twist

Pour the white brandy into a cocktail glass. Add ice. Top
off with diet tonic and garnish with lemon twist.

Washington

I serving: 2 carbohydrates

An amber-colored brandy works best for this drink.

1½ ounces dry vermouth
¾ ounce brandy
½ teaspoon Splenda
2 dashes Angostura bitters

Add all ingredients into a chilled cocktail glass. Stir.

W.C.T.U.

1 serving: 3 carbohydrates

A pre-Prohibition drink. W.C.T.U. stands for the Women's Christian Temperance Union. This teetotaler organization is still in existence.

1¼ ounces brandy
1¼ ounces dry vermouth
1 dash Angostura bitters
1 dash orange bitters

Add all ingredients into a chilled cocktail glass. Stir.

Zoom

1 serving: 1 carbohydrate

An adult mini-milkshake with a kick.

1½ ounces clear brandy
½ ounce heavy or whipping cream
½ teaspoon Splenda

Half-fill a shaker with ice. Pour in all ingredients. Shake. Strain into an old-fashioned glass.

11
Frozen/Blender Drinks

THERE ARE TWO CAVEATS to consider when making blender drinks, especially since they are often tropical-themed—the use of certain fruits and the addition of spiced or coconut-flavored rums. Especially avoid bananas (well over 50 carbohydrates per cup) and pineapples (close to 20 carbs per cup), and use any of the sugar-free banana- and pineapple-flavored syrups that are now available. You can always bulk up the texture of your drink with a low-carb strawberry or two or a small handful of blueberries, if desired.

Baja Bob's Piña Colada
1 serving: 3 carbohydrates

A dark rum like Meyers will add to the tropical-like taste of this drink.

1½ ounces rum
3 ounces Baja Bob's Pina Colada Mix
1½ cups crushed ice (or four ice cubes)

Combine all ingredients in a blender and blend until smooth. Pour into a collins glass.

Blueberry Chocolate Frozen Latte
1 serving: 1.5 carbohydrates

You won't believe there's less than 2 carbs in this drink!

1 ounce whiskey
1 ounce chilled espresso (strong instant coffee is fine)
1 ounce Da Vinci Sugar Free Blueberry Syrup
4 ounces Hood's Carb Countdown 2% Reduced Fat
Chocolate Dairy Beverage
4 ice cubes

Combine all ingredients in a blender and blend until smooth. Pour into an Irish Coffee mug.

Bombs Away

1 serving: 4 carbohydrates

Why a name like Bombs Away? Three distilled spirits and a generous splash of *LCB* Orange Brandy—that's why!

½ ounce dark rum
½ ounce vodka
½ ounce tequila
½ ounce *LCB* Orange Brandy
3 ounces Campbell's Diet V8 Splash Strawberry Kiwi
1 large strawberry
4 ice cubes

Combine all ingredients in a blender and blend until smooth. Pour into a sour glass.

Chocolate Almond Joy

1 serving: 2 carbohydrates

This drink is very decadent and an easy one to get carried away with. Use caution here.

1½ ounces vodka
8 ounces Hood's Carb Countdown 2% Reduced Fat
Chocolate Dairy Beverage
1 tablespoon Da Vinci Sugar Free Almond Syrup
1 tablespoon Da Vinci Sugar Free Coconut Syrup
6 ice cubes

Combine all ingredients in a blender and blend until smooth. Pour into a collins glass.

Creamy Rumba

1 serving: 2 carbohydrates

The coconut flavoring of the *LCB* Caribbean Rum gives a pleasant tropical character to this low-carb drink.

2 ounces *LCB* Caribbean Rum
2 ounces heavy or whipping cream
1 teaspoon Splenda
4 ice cubes

Combine all ingredients in a blender and blend until smooth. Pour into a sour glass.

Diet V8 Splash Mañana

1 serving: 2.65 carbohydrates

If you don't have the Diet V8 Splash Tropical Blend on hand, reach for any of the other Campbell's Diet V8 Splash products. They're all terrific.

3 ounces Campbell's Diet V8 Splash Tropical Blend
1½ ounces tequila
½ ounce *LCB* Orange Brandy
¾ ounce lime juice
4 ice cubes
1 ounce seltzer water

Add all ingredients except seltzer water into a blender. Blend until smooth.

Pour into a highball glass and add a splash of seltzer water. Stir.

Frozen Daiquiri

1 serving: 2.75 carbohydrates

You might never go back to a daiquiri mix after you've tasted this *LCB* version.

1½ ounces rum
1 tablespoon *LCB* Orange Brandy
1½ ounces lime juice
4 ice cubes

Combine all ingredients in a blender and blend until smooth. Pour into a sour glass.

Frozen Strawberry Daiquiri

1 serving: 3.7 carbohydrates

A variation on a summertime classic. You can substitute 1 ounce of Da Vinci's Sugar Free Strawberry Syrup for the fresh strawberries and Splenda if desired.

1½ ounces light rum
3 large strawberries
1 tablespoon fresh lime juice
½ teaspoon Splenda
4 ice cubes

Combine all ingredients in a blender. Blend until smooth. Pour into a sour glass.

Irish Shake

1 serving: 8.75 carbohydrates

Another adult milkshake. Granted it's higher in carbs than most of the *LCB* mixed drink recipes. You can substitute Hood's Carb Countdown 2% Reduced Fat Chocolate Dairy Beverage for the Breyer's CarbSmart Chocolate Ice Cream if desired.

1 ounce vodka
1 ounce *LCB* Irish Cream
1 ounce whipping or heavy cream
4 ounces Breyer's CarbSmart Chocolate Ice Cream
1 tablespoon Sweet 'N Low Sugar Free
Chocolate Flavored Syrup
2 ice cubes

Add all ingredients into blender. Blend until smooth. Pour into a coupette glass.

Irish Shake II

1 serving: 4.96 carbohydrates

1 ounce vodka
1 ounce *LCB* Irish Cream
4 ounces EAS Advant Edge Carb Control Chocolate
Fudge Shake or Hood's Carb
Countdown 2% Reduced Fat Chocolate Dairy Beverage
1 teaspoon Sweet 'N Low Sugar Free
Chocolate Flavored Syrup
4 ice cubes

Combine all ingredients in a blender. Blend until smooth. Pour into a coupette glass.

LCB Limoncello Slushie

1 serving: 3.4 carbohydrates

Refreshing, palate-cleansing, and potent!

2 ounces *LCB* Limoncello
2 ounces Da Vinci Sugar Free Lemon Lime Syrup
6 ice cubes

Combine all ingredients in a blender. Blend until smooth.
Pour into a coupette glass.

Piña Colada Slushie

1 serving: 1.5 carbohydrates

The richness of the Hood's Carb Countdown 2% Reduced Fat
Milk Beverage makes this an unbelievable low-carb drink.

1 ounce dark rum
4 ounces Hood's Carb Countdown 2% Reduced
Fat Milk Beverage
1 ounce Da Vinci Gourmet Sugar Free Pineapple Syrup
1 ounce Da Vinci Gourmet Sugar Free Coconut Syrup
6 ice cubes

Combine all ingredients in a blender. Blend until smooth.
Pour into a coupette glass.

Red Sky Delight
1 serving: 1.75 carbohydrates

This drink will certainly brighten up your day!

1 ounce tequila
1½ ounces *LCB* Caribbean Rum
4 ounces Campbell's Diet V8 Splash Strawberry Kiwi
½ teaspoon Kool-Aid (any red-colored flavor)
½ teaspoon Splenda
3 ice cubes

Combine all ingredients in a blender. Blend until smooth. Pour into a coupette glass.

Root Beer Slush
1 serving: 1.7 carbohydrates

If you don't have any *LCB* Root Beer Schnapps on hand, add another ounce of vodka to the called-for 1 ounce plus 3 ounces of diet root beer to this blend.

1 ounce vodka
1 ounce *LCB* Root Beer Schnapps
1 ounce Da Vinci Sugar Free Root Beer Syrup
6 ice cubes

Combine all ingredients in a blender and blend until smooth. Pour into a coupette glass.

Strawberry Orange Daiquiri

1 serving: 3.25 carbohydrates

This is another tasty variation of the classic frozen daiquiri.

1½ ounces rum
1 tablespoon *LCB* Orange Brandy
1½ ounces lime juice
1 ounce Da Vinci Sugar Free Orange Syrup
2 large strawberries
4 ice cubes

Combine all ingredients in a blender and blend until smooth. Pour into a sour glass.

Strawberry Slush

1 serving: 3.75 carbohydrates

The riper the strawberries, the more flavorful the drink. If you use frozen strawberries, check the label on the container: In many instances, sugar is added to the berries. Be careful.

1 ounce vodka
1 tablespoon Da Vinci Sugar Free Strawberry Syrup
½ cup fresh strawberries
4 ice cubes

Combine all ingredients in a blender. Blend until smooth. Pour into a coupette glass.

Tropical Freeze
1 serving: 2.25 carbohydrates

Eliminate or double up any one of the Da Vinci Sugar Free Syrups listed to add variety to this drink. Be creative. Be imaginative.

1 ounce dark rum
½ ounce each Da Vinci Sugar Free Banana,
Coconut, and Pineapple Syrup
6 ounces Campbell's Diet V8 Splash Tropical Blend
6 ice cubes

Combine all ingredients in a blender. Blend until smooth. Pour into a coupette glass.

Tropical Mojito
1 serving: < 1 carbohydrate

A drink of early twentieth-century Cuba that has risen from obscurity to a trendy drink of today. The taste of mint is the key to this drink. No doubt this is a distant cousin to the Mint Julep. This drink is a blender version.

1½ ounces dark rum
½ ounce Da Vinci Sugar Free Crème de Menthe
or Peppermint Paddy Syrup
½ ounce Da Vinci Sugar Free Pineapple Syrup
½ ounce Da Vinci Sugar Free Peach Syrup
½ ounce lime juice
1¼ cups crushed ice (or 4 ice cubes)
1 mint leaf or lime wedge

Combine all ingredients in a blender. Blend until smooth. Pour into a coupette glass. Garnish with mint leaf or lime wedge.

Vanilla Orange Smoothie

1 serving: 1.5 carbohydrates

A *LCB* adult version of a dreamsicle ice cream confection.

1 ounce vodka
4 ounces Hood's Carb Countdown 2% Reduced
Fat Milk Beverage
1 ounce Da Vinci Sugar Free Orange Syrup
1 ounce Da Vinci Sugar Free Vanilla Syrup
4 ice cubes

Combine all ingredients in a blender. Blend until smooth. Pour into a coupette glass.

Watermelon Slushie

1 serving: 6.75 carbohydrates

This drink can also substitute for a low-carb dessert during a hot summer evening.

1 ounce vodka
1 ounce *LCB* Peach Schnapps
4 ounces fresh watermelon
½ teaspoon Splenda
3 ice cubes

Combine all ingredients in a blender. Blend until smooth. Pour into a coupette glass.

12
Gin-Based Drinks

I SELDOM DRINK ARDENT SPIRITS, but if I do, it's usually an aromatic gin in a tall glass with diet tonic, plenty of ice, and a wedge of lime—while a hot August sun is beating down on me. There's something about gin and its taste and smell that says "Summer!" After Prohibition in the United States, gin drinkers quickly managed to forget the rotgut that passed as gin during the "dry" era and gin sales took off until vodka entered the market.

Gin begins as a grain neutral spirit, just like any other grain-based booze. American-made gins usually have a grain bill consisting almost solely of corn and are distilled to a high proof. In England, the typical gin is derived from corn, barley, and other cereal grains and distilled to a lower proof. The unique flavor and aroma of gin occurs when the neutral spirit is distilled again with the addition of botanicals such as juniper berries, coriander seed, and orange peels, to name just a few.

Since the rise in vodka's popularity, beginning in the late 1940s, gin as a whole has experienced falling sales as a popular clear liquor. Bombay Sapphire Gin from Bacardi is one exception. It has shown steady growth in the last few years. One reason for this overall decline in sales of the aromatic product is the unsophisticated palate of younger drinkers who find the nose and taste of gin to be a bit overwhelming. A comment I've heard often from younger drinkers in the battle between gin and vodka is that they can "taste" gin and prefer vodka because "It doesn't taste like booze." Go figure. A number of gins are going through the same flavoring craze as vodka. Don't be surprised if you see lemon- or lime-flavored gin on the shelves of your favorite liquor store.

0 carbs in gin.

Abbey Cocktail

1 serving: < 1 carbohydrate

No gin on hand? Use vodka and tell your guest it's an "Abbeytini."

1½ ounces gin
2 ounces Campbell's Diet V8 Splash Tropical Blend
2 dashes *LCB* orange bitters

Half-fill shaker with ice. Add all ingredients. Shake well. Strain into a chilled cocktail glass.

Alexander Cocktail

1 serving: 1 carbohydrate

An Alexander can be made with any distilled product, but historically, the first Alexander was gin-based.

1½ ounces gin
1 ounce Da Vinci Gourmet Sugar Free Chocolate Syrup
1 ounce heavy or whipping cream

Half-fill shaker with ice. Add all ingredients. Shake well. Strain into chilled cocktail glass.

Allies

1 serving: 1.3 carbohydrates

Almost a gin martini.

1 ounce gin
1 ounce dry vermouth
1 dash Angostura bitters

Half-fill shaker with ice. Add all ingredients. Shake well. Strain into cocktail glass.

Artillery Cocktail

1 serving: 3.2 carbohydrates

Another variation of a martini drink using sweet vermouth.

1½ ounces gin
½ ounce sweet vermouth
2 dashes Angostura bitters

Half-fill shaker with ice. Add all ingredients. Shake well. Strain into chilled cocktail glass.

Barbary Coast
1 serving: < 1 carbohydrate

If you swear you don't like gin, try this mixed drink and then reconsider.

1 ounce gin
½ ounce Scotch
½ ounce rum
1 tablespoon Da Vinci Gourmet Sugar Free
Chocolate Syrup
½ ounce heavy or whipping cream

Half-fill shaker with ice. Add all ingredients. Shake well. Strain into chilled cocktail glass.

Billy Taylor
1 serving: 1.35 carbohydrates

Another summertime refresher.

2 ounces gin
½ ounce lime juice
6 ounces seltzer or soda water

Fill collins glass with ice. Add gin and lime juice. Top with seltzer or soda water and stir.

Bronx Splash

1 serving: 2.55 carbohydrates

This is a variation on the Bronx Cocktail made with orange juice. Diet V8 Splash works just as well in this *LCB* interpretation.

1 ounce gin
¼ ounce dry vermouth
¼ ounce sweet vermouth
2 ounces Campbell's Diet V8 Splash Tropical Blend

Half-fill shaker with ice. Add all ingredients. Shake well. Strain into a chilled cocktail glass.

Gibson

1 serving: < 1 carbohydrate

A classic drink purportedly invented for American artist Charles Dana Gibson at the Player's Club in New York. A cocktail onion was used since the bar was out of olives.

2½ ounces gin
2 dashes dry vermouth
1 cocktail onion

Half-fill shaker with ice. Add gin and vermouth. Shake well. Strain into chilled cocktail glass. Add onion.

Gimlet
1 serving: 3.15 carbohydrates

Though vodka can also be used in a Gimlet, this classic 1930s drink began as a gin-based predinner drink.

2 ounces gin
1 ounce lime juice
½ teaspoon Splenda
1 lime wedge

Half-fill shaker with ice. Add all ingredients except lime wedge. Shake well. Strain into a chilled cocktail glass. Add lime wedge.

Gin Buck
1 serving: 2.5 carbohydrates

A refreshing summertime drink.

1½ ounces gin
1 ounce lemon juice
4 ounces diet ginger ale

Pour gin and lemon juice into a highball glass filled with ice. Top off with diet ginger ale. Stir.

Gin Cobbler

1 serving: 1.25 carbohydrates

Don't have any gin on hand? Any liquor will work in this classic mixed drink.

2 ounces gin
1/2 ounce lemon juice
1 teaspoon Splenda
4 ounces seltzer or club soda
1 lemon or lime wedge

Pour gin, lemon juice, Splenda, and a splash of seltzer or soda water into shaker. Shake well. Pour into a highball glass.

Add ice and top off with more seltzer or soda water. Garnish with lemon or lime wedge.

Gin Rickey

1 serving: 1.35 carbohydrates

This classic highball recipe is receptive to any liquor.

1 1/2 ounces gin
1/2 ounce lime juice
4 ounces seltzer or club soda
1 lime wedge

Fill highball glass with ice. Pour in gin and lime juice.

Top off with seltzer or club soda. Stir gently. Garnish with lime wedge.

Gin Smash

1 serving: 2.65 carbohydrates

Distantly related to a Mint Julep. Try bourbon or whiskey if you're out of gin.

2 fresh mint leaves
2 ounces gin
1 ounce lemon juice
4 ounces seltzer or club soda
1 lemon slice

Muddle mint leaves with the back of a spoon on the bottom of an old-fashioned glass.

Pour in gin and lemon juice. Add ice and top off with seltzer or club soda. Stir. Garnish with lemon slice.

Leap Frog

1 serving: < 1 carbohydrate

Another highball-type drink that can also be made using vodka.

1½ ounces gin
1 dash lemon juice
4 ounces diet ginger ale

Combine all ingredients in an old-fashioned glass. Add ice. Stir.

Princeton Cocktail

1 serving: 3.05 carbohydrates

Almost a classic gin martini recipe.

2 ounces gin
½ ounce dry vermouth
1 ounce lime juice

Half-fill shaker with ice. Add all ingredients. Shake well. Strain into chilled cocktail glass.

13

Hot Drinks

THOUGHT OF MOST OFTEN, perhaps, as cold-weather drinks, sweet and rich hot drinks can be a great accompaniment to any dessert item or even featured as the dessert itself.

In most cases, these drinks are prepared in heat-resistant glasses or mugs. Whether making punches, toddies, grogs, or nogs, never heat whatever spirit is called for or you might burn off the embracing effects of the alcohol. The whole genre of alcoholic drinks has come a long way from their early origins. Without the convenience of gas or electric stoves or microwave ovens in years long gone, these drinks were usually heated by plunging a red-hot poker from a nearby fireplace into them.

Brandy Toddy
1 serving: 1.5 carbohydrates

In my mind, this is a winter bracer. Substitute whiskey if brandy isn't available.

2 ounces brandy
½ ounce lemon juice
½ teaspoon Splenda
6 ounces hot water
1 lemon twist
1 dash nutmeg

Preheat an Irish coffee glass or a standard coffee mug by pouring in boiling water and letting it sit for one minute. Empty goblet.

Pour in all ingredients except lemon twist and nutmeg. Stir. Garnish with lemon twist. Dust top with a dash of ground nutmeg.

French Coffee
1 serving: 2.5 carbohydrates

You can double up the *LCB* Orange Brandy in this drink if desired.

½ ounce *LCB* Orange Brandy
4 ounces hot black coffee
1 teaspoon Splenda
2 ounces heavy or whipping cream

Whip cream in a chilled container until consistency is thick.

In a standard coffee mug, add *LCB* Orange Brandy, coffee, and Splenda. Stir to dissolve Splenda.

Top off with a generous dollop of the whipped cream.

Gorilla Sweat

1 serving: < 1 carbohydrate

Be sure to use sweet—and not salted butter—in this hot drink. And please, don't even think of using margarine.

1½ ounces tequila
½ teaspoon Splenda
5 ounces boiling water
1 pat unsalted butter
1 cinnamon stick

In a standard coffee mug, add tequila and Splenda. Stir.

Add boiling water. Stir well. Float butter on top. Stir with cinnamon stick.

Hot Buttered Rum

1 serving: 1.75 carbohydrates

A cold-weather classic.

2 ounces dark rum
2 teaspoons Splenda
2 cloves
4 ounces boiling water
1 teaspoon unsalted butter
1 cinnamon stick

In a standard coffee mug, add rum, Splenda, and cloves. Stir.

Add boiling water. Float butter on top and stir with cinnamon stick.

Hot Eggnog
I serving: 4.3 carbohydrates

No pasteurized eggs available? Use 2 tablespoons of packaged and pourable egg substitute.

1 pasteurized egg
1 teaspoon Splenda
1 ounce brandy
½ ounce rum
5 ounces heavy or whipping cream, heated (not boiling)
1 dash nutmeg

In an Irish Coffee goblet, vigorously beat egg and Splenda together.

Pour in brandy and rum. Top off with heated cream. Stir.

Float a dash of nutmeg on top.

Hot Toddy
I serving: 1.9 carbohydrates

A variation of the Gorilla Sweat above.

2 ounces whiskey
1 teaspoon Splenda
5 ounces boiling water
1 teaspoon unsalted butter
2 dashes cinnamon

In a standard coffee mug, add whiskey and Splenda. Stir.

Add boiling water. Stir well.

Float butter on top and sprinkle with cinnamon.

Irish Coffee
I serving: 2.15 carbohydrates

Add a drop or two of *LCB* Mexican Coffee Liqueur into the heavy cream before whipping for a sophisticated touch to this classic drink.

1 ounce Irish whiskey
4 ounces hot black coffee
1 teaspoon Splenda
2 ounces heavy or whipping cream

Preheat an Irish coffee goblet or a standard coffee mug by pouring in boiling water and letting it sit for one minute.

Whip cream in a chilled container until consistency is thick. Empty goblet or coffee mug of heated water and add whiskey, coffee, and Splenda. Stir to dissolve Splenda.

Top off with a dollop of the whipped cream.

Jamaican Coffee
I serving: 4.15 carbohydrates

Use Meyer or Mount Gay dark rum for added authenticity.

1 ounce dark rum
³⁄₄ ounce *LCB* Caribbean Coffee Liqueur
1 teaspoon Splenda
4 ounces hot coffee
2 ounces heavy or whipping cream

Whip cream in a chilled container until consistency is thick.

Pour coffee, dark rum, *LCB* Caribbean Coffee Liqueur into a standard coffee mug. Add Splenda. Stir to dissolve.

Top off with a dollop of the whipped cream.

Mexican Coffee
1 serving: 1.25 carbohydrates

A clear or gold tequila works well in this hot drink.

1½ ounces tequila
1 teaspoon Splenda
4 ounces hot coffee
¼ ounce *LCB* Mexican Coffee Liqueur

In a standard coffee mug, pour in tequila and Splenda. Stir.
Add hot coffee. Float *LCB* Mexican Coffee Liqueur on top.

Russian Coffee
1 serving: 2.15 carbohydrates

Stoli vodka adds a nice touch to this drink.

1½ ounces vodka
1 teaspoon Splenda
4 ounces hot coffee
2 ounces heavy or whipping cream

Whip cream in a chilled container until consistency is thick.
In a standard coffee mug, add vodka, Splenda, and coffee.
Stir to dissolve Splenda.
Top off with a generous dollop of the whipped cream.

14

Rum-Based Drinks

ALTHOUGH RUM MIGHT BE THE OLDEST distilled spirit in the world, it's also become the hottest contemporary liquor in popularity. From the clear rum products with their almost vodka-like tastes, to the darkest rums, ideal for tropical-type drinks, they all are slowly being pushed aside with the steady growth of the flavored and spiced rum categories.

For some LC dieters, it's a liquor to be avoided. Why? Because of the mistaken notion that all rums contain sugar. Rum comes either from the juices of sugar cane or the cheaper by-product of extracting sugar from cane, called molasses. It does rely on a sugary base as a source of fermentation, but so do all distilled products. After fermentation, the murky liquid averages an alcoholic strength of about 7%. Distillation holds the key to leaving any residual carbohydrates behind and bringing the liquor up to a higher proof. As mentioned earlier, rums can then be either bottled with no aging or allowed to mellow and darken in wood barrels for an extended period of time. In terms of sales, clear, young rums are consistent winners. I think a big reason for this is that the darker rums, like gin, are too flavorful for younger palates.

0 carbs in nonspiced or flavored rums.

Adios Amigos

1 serving: 1.25 carbohydrates

Another variation of this mixed drink using rum rather than tequila.

1 ounce light rum
½ ounce dry vermouth
½ ounce brandy
½ ounce gin
½ ounce lime juice

Half-fill shaker with ice. Add all ingredients. Shake. Strain into a cocktail glass.

Black Devil

1 serving: < 1 carbohydrate

Similar in taste to a vodka martini—and just as potent!

1½ ounces light rum
½ ounce dry vermouth
1 black olive

Mix rum and dry vermouth in a cocktail glass. Add ice. Garnish with black olive.

Creole
I serving: < I carbohydrate

Bam! Garnish with a fresh okra pod to add a touch of New Orleans authenticity.

1½ ounces light rum
1 teaspoon lemon juice
2 dashes Tabasco sauce
1 dash Worcestershire sauce
4 ounces beef bouillon
Salt and pepper, to taste

Pour all ingredients into a chilled old-fashioned glass. Stir. Add ice, salt, and pepper to taste. Stir again.

Cuba Libre (Rum and Coke)
I serving: 2.7 carbohydrates

Light Bacardi is the original rum to be used here.

2 ounces light rum
1 ounce lime juice
4 ounces Diet Coke
1 lime wedge

Mix rum, lime juice, and Diet Coke into a highball glass. Add ice and garnish with lime wedge.

Daiquiri

1 serving: 3 carbohydrates

Forget those daiquiri mixes. This is a real homemade and tasty *LCB* effort.

2 ounces light rum
1 ounce lime juice
1 teaspoon Splenda

Half-fill shaker with ice. Add all ingredients. Shake well. Strain into a chilled cocktail glass.

Hat Trick

1 serving: 2.2 carbohydrates

If you don't have dark rum on hand, double up the called-for light rum.

½ ounce dark rum
½ ounce sweet vermouth
½ ounce light rum

Half-fill shaker with ice. Add all ingredients. Shake well. Strain into chilled cocktail glass.

Havana Cocktail

1 serving: < 1 carbohydrate

Another mixed drink that proves that the Diet V8 Splash products can make anyone a *Low-Carb Bartender*.

1 ounce light rum
1½ ounces Campbell's Diet V8 Splash Tropical Blend
1 dash Rose's Lime Juice

Fill shaker with ice. Add all ingredients. Shake well. Strain into a chilled cocktail glass.

Hurricane

1 serving: 3.75 carbohydrates

You can reduce the amount of rum this drink calls for, if desired, but a typical New Orleans Hurricane is strong, strong, strong!

3 ounces dark rum
6 ounces Campbell's Diet V8 Splash Berry Blend
1 ounce lemon juice
1 orange slice

Fill shaker with ice. Add all ingredients. Shake well.
Strain into a chilled hurricane glass. Garnish with orange slice. Sip through a straw.

Mojito

l serving: 4.5 carbohydrates

If you look closely at this recipe, you'll see that it's related to the American Mint Julep.

6 mint leaves
1 tablespoon *LCB* Simple Syrup
1 tablespoon lime juice
1½ ounces light rum
6 ounces seltzer or club soda
1 mint sprig

Add mint leaves and *LCB* Simple Syrup into a collins glass. Use a long spoon to muddle the leaves a bit. Swirl the mixture in the glass.

Add lime juice. If using fresh juice, toss lime shell into glass after releasing juice. Add rum, then ice.

Top off with seltzer or club soda and stir gently. Garnish with mint sprig.

Planter's Splash

1 serving: 2.1 carbohydrates

The original Planter's Punch was created in 1879 to celebrate the opening of Meyer's Rum distillery in Jamaica. Once again, Diet V8 Splash comes to the rescue, substituting for the normally called-for orange juice.

2 ounces dark rum
3 ounces Campbell's Diet V8 Splash Tropical Blend
½ ounce lemon juice
½ teaspoon Splenda
4 ounces seltzer or soda water

Half-fill a collins glass with ice. Add all ingredients except seltzer or soda water. Stir.

Top off with seltzer or soda water. Stir.

Platinum Blonde

1 serving: < 1 carbohydrate

Not sure of the origin of this drink's name, but this Platinum Blonde goes down easy.

1½ ounces light rum
½ ounce heavy or whipping cream
1 tablespoon Da Vinci Sugar Free Orange Syrup

Half-fill a shaker with ice. Pour in all ingredients. Shake. Strain into a cocktail glass.

Rum Highball

I serving: <1 carbohydrate

All highballs have three things in common: They use one liquor, one mix, and can be quickly made.

2 ounces light rum
4 ounces diet ginger ale

Combine all ingredients in a highball glass. Add ice. Stir.

Rum Sour

I serving: 2.95 carbohydrates

A sour is another chameleon-type mixed drink that can adapt to virtually any distilled liquor.

2 ounces light rum
1 ounce lemon juice
1 teaspoon Splenda

Half-fill shaker with ice. Add all ingredients. Shake well. Strain into a sour glass.

Rum Splashdriver

1 serving: 1.88 carbohydrates

The orange juice "screw" has been dropped from this recipe and replaced with the versatile Diet V8 Splash. Be sure to try this drink using vodka, too!

2 ounces dark rum
5 ounces Campbell's Diet V8 Splash Tropical Blend

Combine all ingredients in a highball glass. Add ice. Stir.

Rum Swizzle

1 serving: 3.15 carbohydrates

Swizzles can hold up to any distilled spirit. Rum takes its turn here.

2 ounces light rum
1 ounce lime juice
1 teaspoon Splenda
2 dashes Angostura bitters
4 ounces seltzer or club soda

Combine all ingredients into a highball glass. Add ice. Stir.

15
Tequila-Based Drinks

THOUGH THE POPULARITY OF TEQUILA has declined slightly in the last few years, it's still a popular liquor that lends itself to many mixed drink recipes. If you're using this south-of-the-border made spirit in mixed drinks, use the cheaper, young, clear, or gold products. For a little added taste, the darker colored *reposado* tequilas will also work. For straight sipping—like a fine cognac—*anejo* is most recommended. It would be a shame to pour this complex aged spirit into a sweet and diluted base.

0 carbs in tequila.

Bloody Maria

1 serving: 4.25 carbohydrates

A south-of-the-border takeoff on the vodka-inspired Bloody Mary.

1½ ounces tequila
1 pinch celery salt
1 pinch pepper
1 dash Worcestershire sauce
2 dashes Tabasco sauce
1 lime wedge
4 ounces tomato juice

In a double old-fashioned glass, pour in tequila. Add celery salt, pepper, Worcestershire sauce, and Tabasco.

Squeeze juice of the lime wedge into mixture. Toss in the lime wedge. Add ice.

Top off with tomato juice. Stir.

Mano y Mano

1 serving: 5 carbohydrates

Be sure to pace yourself here.

1 lime wedge
Salt
1½ ounces tequila
12 ounces Corona Light

Squeeze a little lime juice on the top of your hand between your thumb and first finger. Sprinkle salt on moist area.

Drink jigger of tequila in one gulp. Lick salt from your hand. Suck the remaining juice from the lime wedge.

Follow up with the Corona Light, straight from the bottle.

Mexican Banger

1 serving: 3.3 carbohydrates

A tequila takeoff on a Harvey Wallbanger.

1½ ounces tequila
6 ounces Diet V8 Splash Tropical Blend
½ ounce *LCB* Italiano Liqueur

Fill a collins glass with ice. Pour in tequila and Diet V8 Splash. Stir.

Float *LCB* Italiano Liqueur on top.

Mexican Splash

1 serving: 2.3 carbohydrates

If you find the taste of tequila somewhat challenging, keep a bottle in your freezer. It will go down smoother.

1½ ounces tequila
6 ounces Campbell's Diet V8 Splash Strawberry Kiwi
1 lime wedge

Fill a collins glass with ice. Pour in tequila and Diet V8 Splash. Stir. Add ice. Garnish with lime wedge.

Peachy Almond Milkshake

1 serving: 2.75 carbohydrates

Another adult milkshake that goes down easy—maybe too easy!

1½ ounces tequila
1 ounce Da Vinci Sugar Free Almond Syrup
1 ounce Da Vinci Sugar Free Peach Syrup
6 ounces Hood's Carb Countdown 2% Reduced Fat Milk
Beverage
6 ice cubes

Combine all ingredients in a blender and blend until smooth. Pour into a collins glass.

Sourteq

1 serving: 2.65 carbohydrates

Another one of the versatile sour-based drinks. Don't care for tequila? Any spirit will work here.

1½ ounces tequila
1 ounce lemon juice
½ teaspoon Splenda

Half-fill shaker with ice. Add all ingredients. Shake well. Strain into a sour glass. Add ice.

Splenteq
1 serving: 2.75 carbohydrates

Remember—use a clear or slightly aged *reposado* tequila in your mixed drinks. Save your bottle of *anejo* for smooth low-carb sipping, just like a fine cognac.

1 ounce tequila
1 ounce *LCB* Italiano Liqueur
1 ounce Campbell's Diet V8 Splash Tropical Blend
1 lime wedge
1 teaspoon Splenda
1 pinch cinnamon

Half-fill shaker with ice. Pour in tequila, *LCB* Italiano Liqueur, and Diet V8 Splash. Shake.

Rub the lime wedge around the rim of a cocktail glass. Combine Splenda and cinnamon on a paper plate.

Twirl glass around mixture to pick up a coating on the rim of the glass.

Strain shaker contents into a cocktail glass.

Teggim

1 serving: 2 carbohydrates

Don't have any Rose's Lime Juice on hand? Use the juice of a lime wedge and ½ teaspoon of Splenda instead. Then go out and buy some Rose's.

1 ounce tequila
1 teaspoon Rose's Lime Juice

In a highball glass, add both ingredients. Stir. Add ice.

Tequila Collins

1 serving: 2.95 carbohydrates

The versatile collins base meets tequila. The original collins was a gin-based drink, but has evolved to accommodate all spirits.

1½ ounces tequila
1 ounce lemon juice
1 teaspoon Splenda
4 ounces seltzer or soda water

Half-fill shaker with ice. Add all ingredients except seltzer or soda water. Shake well.

Strain into a collins glass. Add ice. Top off with seltzer or soda water. Stir.

Tequila Fizz

1 serving: 2.2 carbohydrates

Try your choice of booze in this drink if tequila isn't on hand.

1½ ounces tequila
1 ounce lemon juice
½ teaspoon Splenda
1 dash Angostura bitters
6 ounces seltzer or soda water

Add all ingredients except seltzer or soda water into a collins glass. Add ice. Top off with seltzer or soda water. Stir.

Tequila Mano

1 serving: < 1 carbohydrate

Be careful!

1 lime wedge
Salt
1½ ounces tequila

Squeeze a little lime juice on the top of your hand between your thumb and first finger.

Sprinkle salt on moist area. Drink jigger of tequila in one gulp. Lick salt from your hand.

Suck the remaining juice from the lime wedge. Repeat.

Tequila Old-Fashioned
1 serving: < 1 carbohydrate

Old-Fashioneds have been around since the early 1900s. This recipe is a contemporary twist.

1½ ounces tequila
½ teaspoon Splenda
1 dash Angostura bitters
2 ounces seltzer or soda water
1 lemon twist

Pour all ingredients except the lemon twist into an old-fashioned glass. Stir.

Add ice. Garnish with lemon twist.

Tequila Rickey
1 serving: 2.65 carbohydrates

The original rickey was gin-based. Vodka, however, seems to be more the liquor of choice in this drink but tequila lends additional variety to this old favorite.

1½ ounces tequila
1 ounce lime juice
4 ounces seltzer or soda water
1 lime wedge

Add tequila and lime juice into a highball glass. Stir.

Add ice and top off with seltzer or soda water. Garnish with lime wedge.

Tequila Sour
1 serving: 2.1 carbohydrates

Another variation of the classic sour-type drink.

1½ ounces tequila
1 ounce lemon juice
½ teaspoon Splenda
1 lemon twist

Half-fill shaker with ice. Pour in tequila, lemon juice, and Splenda. Shake.

Strain into a highball glass. Add ice. Garnish with lemon twist.

Tequila Sunrise
1 serving: 2.3 carbohydrates

This colorful drink is actually a Mexican drink created around the 1930s. Be sure to add the *LCB* grenadine syrup into the glass first.

1½ ounces tequila
6 ounces Campbell's Diet V8 Splash Tropical Blend
1 ounce *LCB* grenadine syrup
1 splash seltzer or soda water

Half-fill shaker with ice. Pour in tequila and Diet V8 Splash.

In a collins glass, add *LCB* grenadine syrup, then a splash of seltzer or soda water. Add ice.

Slowly pour in shaker of tequila and Diet V8 Splash. By adding *LCB* grenadine syrup first in the glass, you should wind up with a "sunrise" effect—and a great tasting drink.

Tequonic

I serving: < I carbohydrate

A variation of the classic gin and tonic.

1 ounce tequila
1 teaspoon lime juice
4 ounces diet tonic water

Add tequila and lime juice to a highball glass. Stir. Add ice. Top off with diet tonic water.

16
Vodka-Based Drinks

BECAUSE OF THE WIDESPREAD LACK of understanding of what actually goes into the fermentable base for vodka as well as the distillation process, vodka has been somewhat canonized by some diet book authors and recommended as the drink of choice in a low-carb diet, but for all the wrong reasons. The fact that it is a clear, neutral spirit might also have something to do with this perception.

This being said, it actually *is* a great liquor for carb counters, and melds effortlessly into virtually any mixed drink base that one can conceive of. The higher the number of distillation and filtering cycles vodka goes through, the smoother it becomes. Throw a bottle into your freezer if you're looking for an even smoother-tasting effect.

0 carbs in straight vodka.

Bloody Bull
1 serving: 2.75 carbohydrates

A variation of the classic Bloody Mary.

1½ ounces vodka
2 ounces beef bouillon
2 ounces tomato juice
2 dashes Worcestershire sauce
2 dashes Tabasco sauce
1 pinch celery salt
1 pinch pepper
1 lemon slice

In a double old-fashioned glass, add all ingredients except lemon slice. Fill with ice. Stir. Garnish with lemon slice.

Bloody Mary
1 serving: 4.55 carbohydrates

Created in the early days of Prohibition, this drink was renamed after Repeal as a "Red Snapper," purportedly because some took offense at the original moniker. When Tabasco sauce was added to the recipe in the 1930s, however, bartenders dropped the politically correct name and went back to calling this tomato and vodka-based drink a Bloody Mary.

1½ ounces vodka
2 dashes Worcestershire sauce
4 dashes Tabasco sauce
4 ounces tomato juice
1 pinch celery salt
1 pinch pepper
1 lemon slice

In an old-fashioned glass, add vodka, Worcestershire sauce, and Tabasco sauce. Fill with ice.

Top off with tomato juice. Stir. Sprinkle with celery salt and pepper. Garnish with lemon slice.

Easy Life
1 serving: < 1 carbohydrate

Deceptively dangerous, but low-carb.

1½ ounces vodka
½ ounce white brandy

Add vodka and brandy into an old-fashioned glass. Add ice. Stir.

Ginka
1 serving: < 1 carbohydrate

Another variation of the classic martini.

1 ounce vodka
1 ounce gin
½ ounce dry vermouth
1 lemon twist

In a chilled cocktail glass, pour in vodka, gin, and dry vermouth. Stir. Garnish with lemon twist.

Golden Splash
1 serving: 2.5 carbohydrates

A clear, young brandy will also work in this recipe.

2 ounces vodka
1 ounce dark brandy
4 ounces Campbell's Diet V8 Splash Tropical Blend

In a collins glass, pour in all ingredients. Add ice. Stir.

Gravel Gertie
1 serving: 1.5 carbohydrates

Don't be put off by the idea of using clam juice in a mixed drink. It adds a nice zing. It's also another hangover "cure."

1 ounce vodka
1 ounce tomato juice
1 ounce clam juice
1 dash Tabasco sauce

Add all ingredients into an old-fashioned glass. Add ice. Stir.

Headless Horseman

1 serving: < 1 carbohydrate

A vodka highball with attitude.

2 ounces vodka
2 dashes Angostura bitters
6 ounces diet ginger ale

Add vodka and bitters into a collins glass. Add ice. Top off
with diet ginger ale. Stir.

Huntsman

1 serving: 2.25 carbohydrates

The unusual combination of vodka and rum works well here
with the addition of lime juice and Splenda.

1½ ounces vodka
½ ounce rum
¾ ounce lime juice
½ teaspoon Splenda

Half-fill shaker with ice. Add all ingredients. Shake well.
Strain into a cocktail glass.

Kangaroo

I serving: < I carbohydrate

Another variation of a vodkatini.

1½ ounces vodka
¾ ounce dry vermouth
1 lemon twist

Pour vodka and vermouth into a chilled cocktail glass. Stir. Garnish with lemon twist.

Kremlin Cooler

I serving: 1.65 carbohydrates

A light-tasting refresher with a kick.

2 ounces vodka
½ ounce lime juice
½ teaspoon Splenda
4 ounces seltzer or soda water

Pour vodka and lime juice into a highball glass. Add Splenda and ice. Top off with seltzer or soda water. Stir.

Sea Breeze

1 serving: 1.5 carbohydrates

Though using carbonated drinks in a cocktail shaker is not normally advised, make an exception here and pick up the sweet and sour taste of grapefruit juice without the carbonation and the carbs.

1½ ounces vodka
2 ounces Old Orchard Apple Cranberry Juice Cocktail
3 ounces Fresca

Half-fill shaker with ice. Pour in all ingredients.

Shake vigorously (to release the carbonation in the Fresca) and strain into an old-fashioned glass filled with ice.

Splashdriver

1 serving: 1.65 carbohydrates

A low-carb alternative to the classic screwdriver.

1½ ounces vodka
5 ounces Campbell's Diet V8 Splash, any flavor

Fill collins glass with ice. Pour in vodka and top off with Diet V8 Splash. Stir.

Twister

1 serving: 2.7 carbohydrates

If you don't have Diet 7 Up on hand, use any sugar-free lemon-lime soda.

2 ounces vodka
1 ounce lime juice
5 ounces Diet 7 Up

Fill collins glass with ice. Pour in vodka. Add lime juice. Top off with Diet 7 Up. Stir.

Vodka and Tonic

1 serving: 2.25 carbohydrates

Originally a gin-based drink.

1½ ounces vodka
1 ounce lime juice
6 ounces diet tonic
1 lime wedge

Fill collins glass with ice. Pour in vodka.

Add lime juice. Top off with diet tonic. Stir. Garnish with lime wedge.

Vodka Collins
1 serving: 2 carbohydrates

In this collins drink, vodka is the liquor of choice. Remember, though, that a collins-type recipe can accommodate any liquor.

1½ ounces vodka
1 ounce lemon juice
6 ounces seltzer or soda water
1 lemon slice

Fill collins glass with ice. Pour in vodka.

Add lemon juice. Top off with seltzer or soda water. Stir. Garnish with lemon slice.

17
Whiskey- (or Whisky-) Based Drinks

"WHISKEY" IS A SOMEWHAT GENERIC TERM that encompasses bourbon, blends, Tennessee whiskey (sour mash), rye, light, Canadian whisky, Scotch, and Irish whiskey. The differences can usually be accounted for by the kind of still used in the distillation process, various combinations of grains used in the mash, the length of aging, blending techniques, and different proof levels of the finished product. Whiskey, like other grain-based spirits, begins as a clear product that takes on its characteristic color through aging in oak barrels or charred oak barrels (as with bourbon).

You might have noticed the two different spellings of whiskey/whisky. The term "whiskey" is shared by the United States and Ireland, while Canada and Scotland drop the "e" from the word. Just one of life's little peculiarities. The only exception to this quirk in spelling can be seen on the Maker's Mark brand of bourbon. At one point in its early history, an exception was made by the federal government to allow this bourbon's label to use the term "whisky" rather than the Americanized "whiskey." It's claimed that this exception was made after the insistence of the original owner and distiller, T. W. Samuels, to be allowed to pay respect to his Scottish heritage.

0 carbs in whiskey.

Admiral Cocktail

1 serving: 2.5 carbohydrates

Almost a dry Manhattan.

1½ ounces whiskey
½ ounce dry vermouth
¾ ounce lemon juice

Half-fill shaker with ice. Add all ingredients. Shake well. Strain into a cocktail glass.

Algonquin

1 serving: 1.2 carbohydrates

If you don't have the Tropical Blend of Diet V8 Splash on hand, try Campbell's other selections of this low-carb fruit drink.

1½ ounces whiskey
¾ ounce dry vermouth
1 ounce Campbell's Diet V8 Splash Tropical Blend

Half-fill shaker with ice. Pour in all ingredients. Shake. Strain into a cocktail glass.

Amaranth

1 serving: 1.5 carbohydrates

A refreshing drink with a hint of low-carb sweetness.

1½ ounces whiskey
2 dashes Angostura bitters
1 teaspoon Splenda
4 ounces seltzer or soda water

Combine whiskey, bitters, and Splenda in a highball glass. Stir. Add ice. Top with seltzer or soda water. Stir.

Bianco

1 serving: < 1 carbohydrate

Another variation of the classic dry Manhattan.

1½ ounces whiskey
½ ounce dry vermouth
1 dash Angostura bitters
1 lemon twist

Combine whiskey and dry vermouth in a highball glass. Stir. Add ice. Top with a dash of bitters. Garnish with lemon twist.

Bordever

1 serving: < 1 carbohydrate

Add more diet ginger ale to this recipe if so desired.

2 ounces whiskey
1 ounce diet ginger ale
1 lemon twist

Combine whiskey and diet ginger ale in a highball glass. Stir. Add ice. Garnish with lemon twist.

Cablegram

1 serving: 1.5 carbohydrates

Note that diet ginger ale goes into the highball glass after the other ingredients get a good shaking in a cocktail shaker. You don't want to lose the effervescence of the diet ginger ale by shaking out all the bubbles.

1½ ounces whiskey
½ ounce lemon juice
½ teaspoon Splenda
4 ounces diet ginger ale
1 lemon twist

Half-fill shaker with ice. Add whiskey, lemon juice, and Splenda. Shake well.

Strain into a highball glass with ice. Top off with diet ginger ale. Stir. Garnish with lemon twist.

Canadian Salad

I serving: 2 carbohydrates

Everything but the kitchen sink! Remember that the orange slice is an attractive garnish—and no more.

1 ounce Canadian whisky
½ ounce brandy
½ ounce *LCB* Scotch Honey Whisky
1 ounce Campbell's Diet V8 Splash Tropical Blend
½ ounce lemon juice
½ teaspoon Splenda
1 thin orange slice

Half-fill shaker with ice. Add all ingredients except orange slice. Shake.

Strain into an old-fashioned glass filled with ice. Garnish with orange slice.

Chicago Manhattan

I serving: 2.25 carbohydrates

A variation of a sweet Manhattan.

2 ounces whiskey
½ ounce sweet vermouth
1 dash Angostura bitters
1 strawberry

Half-fill shaker with ice. Pour in all ingredients except strawberry. Shake.

Strain into a cocktail glass. Garnish with strawberry.

Commodore

1 serving: 1.5 carbohydrates

If you have it on hand, substitute 1½ ounces of *LCB* sweet and sour mix for the lemon juice and Splenda.

1½ ounces whiskey
½ ounce lemon juice
½ teaspoon Splenda

Half-fill shaker with ice. Add whiskey, lemon juice, and Splenda. Shake well.

Strain into a cocktail glass with ice.

Dry Manhattan

1 serving: < 1 carbohydrate

A classic—both sweet and dry Manhattans have been around since the 1880s. The dry Manhattan had its heyday in the 1930s.

2 ounces whiskey
¾ ounce dry vermouth
2 dashes Angostura bitters

Half-fill mixing glass with ice. Pour in whiskey and dry vermouth. Add dashes of bitters. Stir.

Fancy Whiskey

1 serving: < 1 carbohydrate

Another "fancy"-type drink, indicated by the addition of a sweet liqueur to the whiskey.

1½ ounces whiskey
½ ounce *LCB* Orange Brandy
1 dash Angostura bitters

Pour all ingredients into an old-fashioned glass. Stir. Add ice.

Faux Scrumpy

1 serving: 4.5 carbohydrates

You can also warm up the apple juice here, pour it into a coffee mug, and add the whiskey to it. Use your imagination!

1 ounce whiskey
6 ounces Old Orchard LoCarb Apple Juice Cocktail

Fill highball glass with ice. Pour in ingredients. Stir.

Greathead

1 serving: < 1 carbohydrate

A variation on the martini.

1 ounce whiskey
½ ounce vodka
1 ounce Old Orchard LoCarb Apple Juice Cocktail

Half-fill an English pint glass or a mixing glass with ice. Pour in all ingredients. Stir.

Strain into a chilled cocktail glass.

Horse Feathers

1 serving: < 1 carbohydrate

This is another highball-type drink.

2 ounces whiskey
6 ounces diet ginger ale
2 dashes Angostura bitters

Fill highball glass with ice. Pour in all ingredients. Stir.

Preakness

1 serving: 4.5 carbohydrates

Don't be afraid of adding the liqueur, Benedictine, to this drink.
Half an ounce is only 2.5 carbohydrates.

1 ounce whisky
½ ounce Benedictine
½ ounce brandy
½ ounce sweet vermouth
1 dash Angostura bitters
1 lemon twist

Half-fill an English pint glass or a mixing glass with ice. Pour
in all ingredients except the lemon twist. Stir.

Strain into a chilled cocktail glass. Garnish with the lemon
twist.

Presbyterian
1 serving: < 1 carbohydrate

Not as saintly as you might think!

2 ounces whiskey
2 ounces diet ginger ale
2 ounces seltzer or club soda
1 lemon twist

Fill highball glass with ice. Pour in whiskey, diet ginger ale, and seltzer or club soda. Stir. Garnish with lemon twist.

San Francisco Treat
1 serving: 4 carbohydrates

The blending of two low-carb fruit drinks adds a nice sweet treat to this concoction.

1½ ounces whiskey
4 ounces Campbell's Diet V8 Splash Tropical Blend
2 ounces Ocean Spray Cranberry Juice Cocktail

Fill highball glass with ice. Pour in all ingredients. Stir.

Spy Catcher
1 serving: < 1 carbohydrate

Be careful here!

1 ounce whiskey
½ ounce *LCB* Sambuca

Pour whiskey and *LCB* Sambuca into a 1½ oz jigger shot glass. Enjoy.

Whiskey and Cola

1 serving: < 1 carbohydrate

An American cousin to the Cuba Libre.

1½ ounces whiskey
6 ounces diet cola
1 lemon wedge

Fill collins glass with ice. Pour in ingredients. Stir. Garnish with lemon wedge.

Whiskey Cooler

1 serving: < 1 carbohydrate

Another low-carb highball.

2 ounces whiskey
6 ounces diet lemon-lime soda
1 lemon wedge

Fill collins glass with ice. Pour in ingredients. Stir. Garnish with lemon wedge.

18

Martinis

THE CENTURY-OLD MARTINI HAS EVOLVED into such a contemporary drink of various guises, that I decided it should have its own chapter. In its original form, the martini was probably known as the "Martinez," a concoction that consisted of bitters, maraschino, vermouth, gin, and ice. The drink was "shaken, not stirred," perhaps indicating that Agent 007 was on to something all along. By the start of the twentieth-century, the now-named "martini" was a mixture of sweet vermouth and gin in equal parts, plus a dash of orange bitters—not quite what most people think of as the "classic" martini, but well on its way.

The harshness of Prohibition-era "bathtub" gin actually gave the classic gin/vermouth martini a boost in popularity. To cover the taste of the gin, two parts of vermouth were added to one part gin, and served up in a chilled glass with a lemon twist. When the 21st Amendment brought back legal booze on December 5, 1933, gin finally returned as a cleaner-tasting spirit. The quantity of vermouth started to decrease in martini recipes, all the better to taste the aromatic gin. The less vermouth, the "drier" the martini became.

The ritual surrounding the practice of how much vermouth goes into a dry martini is never-ending. I've seen bartenders prepared for martini drinkers with a pump-sprayer to simply mist the inside or rim of the cocktail glass with vermouth or use an eyedropper to squeeze off one drop of vermouth. Some barkeepers add a splash of vermouth to the glass, twirl the glass to coat it with the vermouth, pour it out, and then add the gin.

My favorite martini-making observation, however, was years ago in a bar in Michigan City, Indiana. I was standing at the bar next to a retired Chicago politician (who shall remain nameless). He ordered a gin martini and told the barkeeper to pour the gin into the cocktail glass—and then had the confused young man open a bottle of vermouth. The already tipsy politician then commanded that the bar employee "just wave the bottle of vermouth over the glass." Not a drop of vermouth ever left the bottle. Now that's a dry martini!

But where did the contemporary vodka martini come from? It has become such a matter of routine that vodka, rather than gin, is customarily poured into a martini, unless the customer (almost always over age fifty) specifies that he or she actually wants a gin martini. Drink historians (yes, there are people who study the evolution and art of drinking and drink-making) claim that writer Ian Fleming's James Bond character and his insistence on a vodka martini, shaken and not stirred, started the popularity of the "vodkatini." Of course, there are purists who insist that shaking a martini "bruises" it. Bond had a license to kill so he got what he wanted from his bartenders, bruised martini or not.

It's vodka's purported neutral taste and smell, however, that seem to have led to a never-ending tweak to the traditional gin martini recipe, that and the addition of all kinds of colorful and flavorful accompaniments to the clear base.

A blend of gin-based classics, contemporary examples, and the newest recipe trends follows.

Apple Punchtini
1 serving: 2.5 carbohydrates

Be sure to check out the Da Vinci Web site to discover the wide range of sugar-free syrups they have available. Their products are the basis of many of these flavored martinis.

1 ounce vodka
½ ounce clear brandy
¼ ounce Da Vinci Sugar Free Orange Syrup
½ ounce Da Vinci Sugar Free Green Apple Syrup
2 ounces Ocean Spray Light White Cranberry Juice Drink

Half-fill shaker with ice. Pour in all ingredients. Shake and strain into a chilled cocktail glass.

Banana Breadtini

1 serving: 2 carbohydrates

Who would have thought that a martini could taste this good?

1 ounce vodka
$\frac{1}{2}$ ounce chocolate vodka
$\frac{1}{2}$ ounce Da Vinci Sugar Free Banana Syrup
$\frac{1}{2}$ ounce Da Vinci Sugar Free Cookie Dough Syrup
2 ounces heavy or whipping cream

Half-fill shaker with ice. Pour in all ingredients. Shake and strain into a chilled cocktail glass.

Chicago Martini

1 serving: < 1 carbohydrate

For you traditionalists, this drink should do the trick.

2 ounces gin
$\frac{1}{2}$ ounce Scotch
1 olive

Fill a mixing container with ice. Add gin and Scotch.
Stir and strain into a chilled cocktail glass. Add olive as a garnish.

Chocolatini

1 serving: 5.5 carbohydrates

I had to think twice about this recipe. I came across the Web site for Van Gogh Vodkas (*www.vangoghvodka.com*) and was intrigued by the company's lineup of flavored vodkas—Wild Appel (it's a Dutch firm), Dutch Chocolate, Vanilla, Raspberry, Oranje, Melon, Citroen, Pineapple, and Coconut. At 70° proof, I was somewhat wary as to whether or not the vodka was sweetened. After calling the company's customer service number (1-888-539-3361) and asking about the carb counts of their array of flavored vodkas, I'm happy to say that they are also carb-free!

Goldenbärr Chocolate Vodka is also to be considered when thinking "chocolate." This brand is a bit higher in proof at 80° than the Van Gogh line but just as flavorful. If you go to *www.goldenbarr.com*, you can order this cocoa-infused and distilled product and have it shipped to you.

1½ ounces chocolate-flavored vodka
½ ounce *LCB* Mexican Coffee Liqueur
½ ounce Da Vinci Sugar Free Chocolate Syrup
2 ounces heavy or whipping cream
½ teaspoon Sweet 'N Low Sugar Free
Chocolate Flavored Syrup

Take a chilled cocktail glass and zig-zag the Sweet 'N Low Sugar Free Chocolate Flavored Syrup into the interior of the glass.

Momentarily place the glass into the freezer. Half-fill cocktail shaker with ice.

Add remainder of ingredients into shaker. Shake and strain into chocolate-lined cocktail glass. Decadent!

Cosmopolitan
1 serving: 1.85 carbohydrates

Considered by some to be a "woman's drink," this sweet but high-octane concoction has also been described as a feminist manifesto in a glass. Watch out, men!

1 ounce vodka
½ ounce *LCB* Orange Liqueur
1 ounce Ocean Spray Light Cranberry Juice Cocktail
1 lime twist

Half-fill shaker with ice. Pour in all ingredients. Shake and strain into a chilled cocktail glass. Garnish with lime twist.

Cranberrytini
1 serving: 1.25 carbohydrates

A great Thanksgiving Day treat.

1½ ounces cranberry vodka
1 ounce Ocean Spray Light Cranberry Juice Cocktail
1 lime twist

Half-fill shaker with ice. Pour in all ingredients.
Shake and strain into a chilled cocktail glass. Garnish with lime twist.

Dry Martini

1 serving: < 1 carbohydrate

The classic martini.

1½ ounces gin
1 dash dry vermouth
2 green olives

Fill a mixing container with ice.

Add gin and dry vermouth. Stir (or shake if you're James Bond) and strain into a chilled cocktail glass.

Add olives, preferably those colossal-sized, bleu cheese-stuffed ones!

Gingerbread Mantini

1 serving: 2.85 carbohydrates

While the kids are making a gingerbread man for the Christmas season, you can be working on one or two of these.

1 ounce vodka
1 ounce *LCB* Irish Cream
2 ounces Hood's Carb Countdown 2% Reduced Fat
Chocolate Dairy Beverage
½ ounce Da Vinci Sugar Free Gingerbread Syrup

Half-fill shaker with ice. Pour in all ingredients. Shake and strain into a chilled cocktail glass.

Italian Martini

1 serving: < 1 carbohydrate

You can add more *LCB* Amaretto if desired. Remember that these *LCB* drink recipes can be tweaked for your own tastes.

1½ ounces vodka
¼ ounce *LCB* Amaretto
1 lemon twist

Pour vodka and *LCB* Amaretto into a mixing glass. Add ice. Strain into a chilled cocktail glass. Garnish with lemon twist.

Italian Martini II

1 serving: < 1 carbohydrate

A variation of the recipe above using the golden-colored *LCB* Italiano Liqueur.

1½ ounces vodka
¼ ounce *LCB* Italiano Liqueur
1 lemon twist

Pour vodka and *LCB* Italiano Liqueur into a mixing glass. Add ice. Stir.
Strain into a chilled cocktail glass. Garnish with lemon twist.

Martini (Medium)

1 serving: 2.6 carbohydrates

A classic.

1½ ounces gin
½ ounce dry vermouth
½ ounce sweet vermouth
1 lemon peel or olive

Pour gin and dry and sweet vermouth into a mixing glass. Add ice. Stir.

Strain into a chilled cocktail glass. Garnish with lemon peel or olive.

Martini (Sweet)

1 serving: 4.4 carbohydrates

Another classic drink using gin instead of vodka.

1½ ounces gin
1 ounce sweet vermouth
1 lemon peel or olive

Pour gin and sweet vermouth over ice cubes in a mixing glass. Stir.

Strain into a chilled cocktail glass. Add lemon peel or olive.

Mint Pie Martini

1 serving: 2.8 carbohydrates

Don't forget that you can substitute any of the Hood's milk products for heavy cream in any recipe.

1½ ounces vodka
½ ounce *LCB* Crème de Menthe
2 ounces heavy or whipping cream
1 mint leaf

Half-fill shaker with ice. Pour in vodka, *LCB* Crème de Menthe, and heavy or whipping cream. Shake well.

Strain into a chilled cocktail glass. Add mint leaf as garnish.

Piña Coladatini

1 serving: 1.5 carbohydrates

Another example of how the Baja Bob products are so low-carb friendly.

1 ounce vodka
½ ounce dark rum
2 ounces Baja Bob's Piña Colada Mix

Half-fill shaker with ice. Pour in vodka, rum, and piña colada mix.

Shake well. Strain into a chilled cocktail glass.

Rumtini

1 serving: < 1 carbohydrate

A spicy twist on the classic gin martini.

2 ounces light rum
2 dashes dry vermouth
1 olive or lemon twist

Pour rum and dry vermouth into a mixing glass. Add ice. Stir.

Strain into a chilled cocktail glass. Garnish with olive or lemon twist.

Strawberrytini

1 serving: 2 carbohydrates

Add another ½ ounce of vodka and 1 tablespoon of Da Vinci Sugar Free Strawberry Syrup if you don't have *LCB* Strawberry Liqueur on hand.

1½ ounces raspberry vodka
1 ounce *LCB* Strawberry Liqueur
1 strawberry

Half-fill shaker with ice. Pour in raspberry vodka and *LCB* Strawberry Liqueur. Shake well.

Strain into a chilled cocktail glass. Add strawberry as garnish.

VeryBerrytini

1 serving: 3.4 carbohydrates

Careful—this one's addictive—and potent!

1½ ounces cranberry vodka
½ ounce *LCB* Strawberry Liqueur
½ ounce *LCB* Blueberry Liqueur
1 strawberry

Half-fill shaker with ice. Pour in cranberry vodka and *LCB* Strawberry and Blueberry Liqueurs. Shake well.

Strain into a chilled cocktail glass. Add strawberry as garnish.

Watermelontini

1 serving: < 1 carbohydrate

A great-tasting late summertime drink.

2 ounces vodka
½ ounce Da Vinci Sugar Free Watermelon Syrup
1 lime twist

Half-fill shaker with ice. Pour in vodka and syrup. Shake well. Strain into a cocktail glass. Garnish with lime twist.

19
FAQs

CONFUSION AND MISINFORMATION reign supreme when it comes to alcohol and low-carbohydrate dieting. If you believe any of the following "untruths," read this section carefully.

Isn't there sugar in rum?

All fermentables begin as a sugary base or are converted from starch to sugar prior to fermentation. Sugar is the element that yeast needs in order to bring you ethyl alcohol, the substance that puts a smile on your face. Whether the fermentation process begins with a sugary base—as in 0 carb rum—or with the results of the mashing of starchy materials like malted barley into a sugary base—as in 0 carb vodka—is irrelevant.

Isn't there sugar in flavored vodkas?

The process of making a typical flavored vodka, such as produced by Smirnoff, is little different in its manufacturing than the process used to make gin. Unfortunately, there has been such a proliferation of flavored vodkas that have come on the market in the last few years that it's becoming hard to say with absolute certainty that "all fla-vored vodkas are sugar-free." A tip-off that a flavored vodka may have added sugar in it is by noting the proof level of the vodka. As a loose rule of thumb—if the proof is less than 70°, be wary. Better yet, stick with big name brands as discussed earlier.

Some wine-related Web sites say that there are no carbohydrates in dry wine. Is this true?

More rubbish from people who have no idea of the mechanics of fermentation. The process of converting sugars to alcohol and carbon dioxide during fermentation is limited by the attenuation of the yeast or the manipula-tion of the fermentation by the vintner. In order for a wine to have no carbohydrates in it, it would have to be pure alcohol, in other words, distilled. Of course at that point, the liquid would no longer be wine, but brandy or cognac. All—and I repeat—all wines, including dry wines, have some residual sugar left behind after the fermentation process. Residual sugar equals carbohydrates. If it were possible to use fermentation to convert a sugary liquid into a drink that was free of carbohydrates, the process of distillation would be a meaningless procedure. Only after distillation, when the resultant liquid is transformed into ethyl alcohol, will a once-fermented liquid become carbohydrate-free.

What's the difference between fermentation and distillation?

This is a great question since most of the confusion as to whether a liquor has residual sugars in it, and as a result, carbohydrates, stems from a lack of understanding in how it is made.

Fermentation

Before a product can be distilled, it must be fermented. However, before a product can be fermented, it must consist of a sugary base. Yeasts only feed on sugar. In the case of beer, vodka, grain alcohol, the various whiskeys, and gin, the starchy interior of the grains must first be converted into sugar. That is the sole purpose of mashing, as explained in the chapter about beer. In the cases of liquors like tequila, rum, or even wine, this step is eliminated since the fermentables already consist of sugar.

The conversion of sugar to ethyl alcohol during fermentation, however, is limited. Sugars consist of complex and simple sugars. As was discussed earlier, yeasts attack simple sugars. Once their job is done, they either fall to the bottom of the fermentation container and go dormant or create an environment high enough in alcoholic strength that they actually die from their own sugar-to-alcohol activity.

Distillation

At this point, whether we're talking about wine being distilled into brandy or cognac, or the fermented runnings from the results of an initial grain mash, the fermented liquid is now heated in a still. Just as when cooking with liquor, the ethyl alcohol in the fermented liquid evaporates and rises to the top of the still, leaving everything else behind—including carbohydrates. A condenser cools the gaseous vapors back into a liquid—ethyl alcohol. With each subsequent redistillation of the raw alcohol, a cleaner and more pure product will evolve.

Is it correct that alcohol is metabolized and turns into sugar in the bloodstream?

Another alcohol and low-carb diet urban legend. Metabolism is the body's process of converting ingested substances to other compounds. Metabolism results in some substances becoming more, and some less, toxic than those originally ingested. Metabolism involves a number of processes, one of which is referred to as oxidation. Through oxidation, alcohol is detoxified and removed from the blood, preventing the alcohol from accumulating and destroying cells and organs. When alcohol is consumed, it passes from the stomach and intestines into the blood. Alcohol is then metabolized by enzymes that break it down into other chemicals. In the liver, an enzyme called alcohol dehydrogenase (ADH) mediates the conversion of alcohol to acetaldehyde. Acetaldehyde is rapidly converted to acetate by other enzymes and is eventually metabolized to carbon dioxide and water. Alcohol is also metabolized in the liver by the enzyme cytochrome. Most of the alcohol consumed is metabolized in the liver, but the small quantity that remains unmetabolized permits alcohol concentration to be measured in breath and urine. As you can see, alcohol is not metabolized into sugar.

If the sugar in wine can ferment into alcohol, does that add sugar alcohols to the wine?

Whoa—information overload! Sugar alcohols such as mannitol, sorbitol, and xylitol, are polyols. Chemically, they are not alcohols, and though they are derived from sugar molecules found in plant products such as fruit, they are not sugars. A chemical process alters the carbohydrates in these plants to form sugar alcohols. You'll often see sugar alcohols used as a low-carb substitute for sugar in foods. Some dieters who eat foods with sugar alcohols as an ingredient complain of a laxative effect. That being said, sugar alcohols are not part of any product that has undergone fermentation.

I've heard that the lower the alcohol in a beer, the less carbs in it.

It's the residual sugars left behind after fermentation that contribute to the majority of carbs in beer. Nonalcoholic (NA) beers are a good example of this. A Beck's Haake NA, for instance, hits 20 carbs per 12-ounce serving! One of the more common ways to brew a nonalcoholic (NA) beer is to stop the fermentation in its earliest stages. What's left behind is a beer with considerably more sugars and carbohydrates than a regular beer.

I've read that the sugar maltose in beer goes directly to the cells in your stomach, thus the so-called beer belly?

This theory is actually promoted in a number of popular low-carb diet books, including one written by a doctor. The real answer in a nutshell? Nonsense! Glucose is the simple sugar that is transported into our cells and then converted to energy by a series of oxidation-reduction reactions. Maltose, as found in beer in trace or in most cases in nondiscernible amounts (go to *www.drinkbeergetthindiet.com* for a sample of beer styles with residual sugar contents), is a disaccharide that consists of two glucose molecules linked in an alpha 1,4 glycosidic bond. Maltose is not absorbed from our intestines. The enzyme maltase converts maltose into a monosaccharide (glucose) before it can be absorbed—that's why the tips of our villi in our proximal small intestine contain enzymes that break disaccharides into monosaccharides—but this is only part of the reason why this "maltose is bad" theory is so silly.

Where then does the popular "beer-belly" scenario fit in? Glucose is typically converted into fat if there is an excess in the blood compared to current metabolic needs, but the idea that maltose, after it is broken down and converted into glucose and absorbed, has some sort of homing radar that leads it directly to the abdomen where it will be converted to fat is a silly argument. To equate beer with pure maltose is an even sillier argument.

As long as you are able to absorb the sugar, it will go wherever it is needed in the body. The real reason for the "beer belly" is that people who develop them are taking in way more carbohydrates than their current metabolic needs, whether drinking beer or not. After knocking off a pizza or a couple of meatball sandwiches—then sitting on the couch the entire weekend—why call that roll around your middle a "beer belly"? Why not call it what it really is—a carbohydrate- or calorie-overload belly?

There's also ongoing research that indicates the fat that accumulates around the mid-body region might also be because of a predisposed genetic trait, in the same way that some people have wider hips or a larger butt.

What's the glycemic index of beer?
I've seen plenty of information that states
the glycemic index (G.I.) of beer is 110.
That's higher than the G.I. of pure glucose!

As far as I can tell, this false assumption of the G.I. of beer is based on a number of untruths that just won't go away, and is an indicator of illogical assumptions by misinformed diet book authors, dieticians, and nutritionists. Michel Montignac, a Frenchman who penned *Je Mange Donc je Maigris* (Eat Yourself Slim) in 1987 seems to have started all of this. This book, and other similar publications that have followed from Monsieur Montignac, demonize beer but canonize wine. How? By making some incredible leaps of faith that beer is composed mainly of maltose, and as a result, has the same glycemic index of maltose. Imagine if I said that a glass of milk with a teaspoon of chocolate syrup in it had the same glycemic index as a glass of pure chocolate syrup. It just doesn't add up.

The idea of a glycemic index for foods has been around since the early 1980s when Professor Thomas Wolever, now at the University of Toronto, began research on the subject with the possibility of using this information to prevent type 2 diabetes. Wolever's research and subsequent testing led to a way to determine the measurable effects of various foods and drinks on the increase of sugar (glucose) in one's bloodstream after ingestion.

Montignac made the claim in his chart of foods with their glycemic indexes that maltose and beer are one and the same in terms of the glycemic index. The fact that maltose is one of the simple sugars eaten by yeasts during fermentation seems to have eluded him—and also a number of contemporary diet book authors who blindy use Montignac's "research" to bolster their argument that light and regular-brewed beers can't be part of a LC diet or controlled-carbohydrate lifestyle because they supposedly have the same G.I. as pure maltose.

Dr. Jennie Brand-Miller, Professor of Human Nutrition in the Human Nutrition Unit, School of Molecular and Microbial Biosciences at the University of Sydney, Australia, has concluded in her studies that beer has little measurable carbohydrates, and as a result, registers zero on the glycemic index. In actuality, wine and liquor also register zero. The doctor's research has been supported by dozens of studies, including some from the Harvard University School of Public Health. Dr. Brand-Miller, who is also the President of the Nutrition Society of Australia, has written extensively about this intriguing form of measurement for blood glucose levels. Her latest book on the subject is titled *The New Glucose Revolution Complete Guide to Glycemic Index Values*.

Will my weight loss stall if I drink?

Yes. Alcohol is utilized by your body before fat, protein, or carbohydrates. Of course, while you're burning alcohol, you are in a temporary stall. Nothing else will be utilized by your body for fuel. Keep in mind, however, that 1½ ounces of alcohol will be burned off in 1 to 2 hours. A 12-ounce beer equals the alcoholic strength of 5 ounces of wine, which equals 1½ ounces of booze. Two drinks, therefore, will slow down your weight loss for 2 to 4 hours—to me, an insignificant amount of time to really worry about. You can make your own choice.

Does wine differ from beer in terms of carbs?

It depends. There are literally thousands of brands of beer and wine, and as you've seen in the carb lists for these beverages, carbohydrates in these products vary. What might be surprising to many is that, ounce for ounce, the carbohydrate count for beer and wine is remarkably similar. The total carbohydrate count lies in what constitutes an "average" serving. For beer, that is 12 ounces—for wine, 5 ounces.

APPENDIX A
Bar Measurements

1 dash = 4 to 5 drops = .002 fluid ounces (U.S.) = .002 fluid ounces (UK)

1 fluid ounce (U.S.) = 1.4 fluid ounces (UK) = 28.35 g = 30 milliliters

12 fluid ounces (U.S.) = 355 milliliters/ccs

1 cup (U.S.) = 8 fluid ounces (U.S.) = 8.32 fluid ounces (UK) = 250 milliliters

½ fresh lemon = ½ to ¾ fluid ounce (U.S.) = .52 to .78 fluid ounce (UK)

½ fresh lime = ½ fluid ounce juice (U.S.) = .52 fluid ounce (UK)

1 jigger = 1.5 fluid ounces (U.S.) = 1.56 fluid ounces (UK)

1 pint (U.S.) = 16 fluid ounces (U.S.) = 16.54 fluid ounces (UK)

1 pony = 1 fluid ounce (U.S.) = 1.4 fluid ounce (UK) = 28.35 grams

1 splash = 1 tablespoon (U.S.) = .80 tablespoon (UK)

1 tablespoon (tbsp) = 3 teaspoons (U.S.) = .80 table- spoon (UK) = 15 milliliters

1 teaspoon (tsp) = ⅛ ounce (U.S.) = 1.07 teaspoons (UK) = 5 milliliters

Products and Web Sites

Brewhaus
www.brewhaus.com
U.S. distributor of Prestige essences by Gert Strand. In an e-mail from Gert, he says, "In most essences there [are] 3 gram[s of] invert sugar (sucrose treated so it splits into fructose and glucose mono sugars) to give some body in the beverage. One can not taste any sweetness from it."

Prestige
The Prestige selection is much more extensive than the Liquor Quik essences.

Contact Information
Brewhaus (America) Inc.
4824 Carolina Trace
Keller, TX 76248
(817) 271-8041
www.brewhaus.com

Da Vinci Gourmet Syrups
www.davincigourmet.com
Maker of sugar-free and regular flavored syrups. Site includes drink recipes that can be tweaked with the addition of spirits.

Contact Information
7224 1st Avenue South
Seattle, WA 98108
Phone: USA–(800) 640-6779
International–(206) 768-7401
Fax: (206) 764-3989
E-mail: *customerservice@davincigourmet.com*
Mon–Fri, 8 A.M.–5 P.M. PST

Specialty Bottle
www.specialtybottle.com
Extensive selection of bottles. No minimum orders.

Specialty Bottle LLC
5215 5th Avenue S
Seattle, WA 98108
Phone: 206-340-0459
Fax: 206-903-0785
E-mail: *service@specialtybottle.com*
Mon–Fri, 8 A.M.–5 P.M. PST

The Low-Carb Bartender
www.LCBartender.com
Updates, additions, and possible corrections to beer, wine, liqueur, and liquor carbohydrate counts. If you are a beer, wine, or spirits manufacturer and would like carbohydrate information for your products listed in subsequent printings of *The Low Carb Bartender*, send your information to *Webmaster@LCBartender.com*. Site also includes a one-stop shop for products listed in this book.

Winemakeri, Inc.
www.winemakeri.com
Manufacturer and distributor of Liquor Quik essences, bottles, corks, labels, etc.

Winemakeri Inc.
739 Windsor Jct. Cross Rd.
Beaverbank, NS, B4G 1G3
CANADA
Phone: (902) 864-0100
Toll-Free: (877) 278-5464 (order desk only)
Fax: (902) 864-5628
Toll-Free Fax: (877) 278-1991 (order desk only)
Hours: M–F, 8 A.M.–5 P.M. AST

Index

A

Abbey Cocktail, 199
Acapulco, 126
Adios Amigos, 176, 215
Admiral Cocktail, 245
Air Mail, 157
Ale, 6
Ale-based drinks, 83–93
Ale Flip, 84
Ale Sangaree, 85
Alexander Cocktail, 199
Algonquin, 245
Allies, 200
Amaranth, 246
Amaretto, 10, 107
Amaretto II, 122–23
Amber Beer Shot, 85
Americana, 157
Anisette Cocktail, 127
Anisette (Pastis), 109
Apple Punchtini, 257
Apricot Brandy, 110
Artillery Cocktail, 200

B

Baja Bob, 18–19
Baja Bob's Piña Colada, 186
Banana Breadtini, 258
Bar stock/supplies, 3–12
Barbary Coast, 201
Barware, 3–6
Beer, 6
    carbohydrates in, 27–31,
        36–82, 271, 275
    glycemic index of, 273–74
    labels, 31–35
    light/lite, 29–30, 35–37

regular-brewed, 30–31
Beer-based drinks, 83–93
Beer bellies, 271–72
Beer Breezer, 86
Beer Breezer II, 86
Beer Buster, 87
Beer Colada, 87
Benedictine, 10
Berliner Weisse, 88
Between the Sheets, 127
Bianco, 246
Billy Taylor, 201
Bitters, 21
Black & Tan, 88
Black Devil, 215
Black pepper, 21
Black Russian, 128
Black Velvet, 89
Blender drinks, 185–95
Blenders, 3–4
Bloody Bull, 234
Bloody Maria, 224
Bloody Mary, 234–35
Blueberry Chocolate Frozen
    Latte, 186
Blueberry Liqueur, 100
Boilermaker, 89
Bombs Away, 187
Bordever, 247
Boscoe, 128
Bottle/can openers, 4
Bottles, 97
Bourble, 129
Bourbon, 15
Bourbon-based drinks, 129–30,
    165–73
Bourbon Cobbler, 166

Bourbon Collins, 166
Bourbon Cooler, 167
Bourbon Fix, 167
Bourbon Highball, 168
Bourbon Lancer, 168
Bourbon Rickey, 169
Bourbon Sour, 169
Bourbon Swizzle, 170
Brandy, 15–16
Brandy Alexander, 177
Brandy and Soda, 179
Brandy-based drinks, 127, 131,
    175–83, 208, 210
Brandy Crusta, 177
Brandy Fix, 178
Brandy Sling, 178
Brandy Sour, 179
Brandy Swizzle, 180
Brandy Toddy, 208
Brandy Up, 180
Brave Bull, 129
Bronx Splash, 202

C

Cablegram, 247
Can Can, 158
Canadian Salad, 248
Canning jars, 97
Carbohydrates
    in beer, 27–31, 36–82, 271,
        275
    in wines, 135–53, 268, 275
Caribbean Coffee, 110–11
Celery salt, 21
Chambord, 10
Champagne, 155–56
Champagne-based drinks, 155–61
Champagne Cocktail, 158
Champagne Cocktail II, 159

Champagne Julep, 159
Cheesecloth, 97
Chicago Manhattan, 248
Chicago Martini, 258
Chocolate Almond Joy, 187
Chocolatini, 259
Cincinnati, 89
Coconut Rum, 111
Coffee filters, 97
Cognac, 15–16
Colanders, 98
Commodore, 249
Cordials
    See also Liqueurs
    making low-carb, 95–123
    types of, 9–12
Corkscrews, 4
Cosmopolitan, 260
Cranberry Liqueur, 102
Cranberrytini, 260
Creamy Rumba, 188
Crème de Menthe, 11, 112
Creole, 216
Cuba Libre (Rum and Coke), 216
Cutting boards, 4

D, E

Da Vinci Sugar Free Syrups,
    23–24
Daiquiris
    Daiquiri, 217
    Frozen Daiquiri, 189
    Frozen Strawberry Daiquiri,
        189
    Strawberry Orange Daiquiri,
        193
Dairy items, 6–7
Demi Panache, 90
Depth Charge, 90

Diet Snapple, 19
Diet V8 Splash, 19–20
Diet V8 Splash Fizz, 160
Diet V8 Splash Mañana, 188
Diet V8 Splash Mimosa, 160
Dirty Mother, 181
Distillation, 269
Distilled water, 98
Dive Bomber, 91
Dog's Nose, 91
Dry Manhattan, 170, 249
Dry Martini, 261
Easy Going, 130
Easy Life, 235
Equipment, for making low-carb
    liqueurs/cordials, 97–99

F

Fancy Bourbon, 130
Fancy Brandy, 131
Faux Scrumpy, 250
Fermentation, 269
Flavored vodkas, 267–68
Fluffy Ruffles, 161
French Coffee, 208
Frozen Daiquiri, 189
Frozen drinks, 185–95
Frozen Strawberry Daiquiri, 189
Funnel, 98

G

Gancy Whiskey, 250
Garnishes, 7
Gibson, 202
Gimlet, 203
Gin, 16
Gin-based drinks, 127,
    197–206, 258, 261, 263
Gin Buck, 203

Gin Cobbler, 204
Gin Rickey, 204
Gin Smash, 205
Gingerbread Mantini, 261
Ginka, 235
Glasses, 7–9
Glycemic index, of beer,
    273–74
Glycerin, 98–99
Golden Splash, 236
Gorilla Sweat, 209
Grand Marnier, 11
Graters, 4
Gravel Gertie, 236
Greathead, 250
Grenadine, 24
Guinness, 59–60

H

Hat Trick, 217
Havana Cocktail, 218
Hazelnut, 112–13
Headless Horseman, 237
Horse Feathers, 251
Hot Buttered Rum, 209
Hot drinks, 207–12
Hot Eggnog, 210
Hot Toddy, 210
Huntsman, 237
Hurricane, 218

I, J, K

Ice, 9
Ice bucket/tongs, 4
Imitation flavorings, 120
Irish Coffee, 211
Irish Cream, 11, 113
Irish Shake, 190
Irish Shake II, 190

Italian Martini, 262
Italian Martini II, 262
Italiano, 114
Itchy Bitchy, 131
Jamaican Coffee, 211
Kahlúa, 11
Kangaroo, 238
Knives, 4
Kremlin Cooler, 238

L

L. G. Cocktail, 92
La Dolce Prima, 132
Labels
  beer, 31–35
  for homemade liqueurs, 99
LCB Limoncello Slushie, 191
Leap Frog, 205
Lemon/lime juice, 19
Limoncello, 104–5
Liqueurs
  Low-Carb Bartender, 95–123
  methods for making, 125–26
  mixed-drinks using, 126–33
  types of, 9–14
Liquor Quik, 105–6, 108
Liquors, 15–18
Low-carbohydrate diets, 1–2

M, N

Manhattans
  Chicago Manhattan, 248
  Dry Manhattan, 249
Mano y Mano, 224
Margarita, 132
Martinis, 255–66
  Apple Punchtini, 257
  Banana Breadtini, 258
  Chicago Martini, 258

Chocolatini, 259
Cosmopolitan, 260
Cranberrytini, 260
Dry Martini, 261
Gingerbread Mantini, 261
Italian Martini, 262
Italian Martini II, 262
Martini (Medium), 263
Martini (Sweet), 263
Mint Pie Martini, 264
Piña Coladatini, 264
Rumtini, 265
Strawberrytini, 265
VeryBerrytini, 266
Watermelontini, 266
McCormick Extracts, 120, 122
Measuring glass, 5
Metro Cocktail, 181
Mexacola, 133
Mexican Banger, 225
Mexican Coffee, 114–15, 212
Mexican Coffee Liqueur, 101
Mexican Splash, 225
Mint Julep, 171
Mint Pie Martini, 264
Mixers, 18–20
Mixing sticks, 5
Mojito, 219
Napkins, 5
Nutmeg, 21

O

Ocean Spray juice drinks, 20
Oh Henry!, 171
Old Orchard LoCarb Juice
  Cocktails, 20
Orange Bitters, 22–23
Orange Brandy, 115

P, Q

Pastis (Anisette), 109
Peach Schnapps, 116
Peachy Almond Milkshake, 226
Pendennis, 172
Pepper mills, 5
Peppermint Schnapps, 11
Piña coladas
    Baja Bob's Piña Colada, 186
    Piña Colada Slushie, 191
    Piña Coladatini, 264
Planter's Splash, 220
Platinum Blonde, 220
Polar Attraction, 182
Preakness, 251
Presbyterian, 252
Princeton Cocktail, 206
Queen's Cousin, 161

R

Radler, 90
Reamer, 5
Red Eye, 92
Red Sky Delight, 192
Red Wine Spritzer, 162
Root Beer Schnapps, 121
Root Beer Slush, 192
Rose's Lime Juice, 24
Rum, 17, 111, 267
Rum and Coke (Cuba Libre), 216
Rum-based drinks, 126, 133,
    186–89, 191–94, 209–11,
    213–22, 265
Rum Highball, 221
Rum Sour, 221
Rum Splashdriver, 222
Rum Swizzle, 222
Rumtini, 265
Russian Coffee, 212

S

Salt, 21
Sambuca, 12, 116–17
San Francisco Treat, 252
Sazerac, 172
Scotch, 15
Scotch Honey Whiskey, 117
Sea Breeze, 239
Seasonings, 21–22
Shakers, 5–6
Shandy, 90
Shot glass, 5
Simple Syrup, 24–25
Skip and Go Naked, 92
Sodas/seltzers, 20
Sourteq, 226
Southern Whiskey, 118
Splashdriver, 239
Splenda, 25
Splenteq, 227
Spoons, 6
Spy Catcher, 252
Stainless steel pots, 99
Strawberry Liqueur, 103
Strawberry Orange Daiquiri,
    193
Strawberry Slush, 193
Strawberrytini, 265
Sugar, 267–68, 270–71
Supplies, 3–12
Sweet and sour mix, 26
Sweeteners, 23–26
Swiss Chocolate Almond,
    118–19

T

Tabasco sauce, 22
Teggim, 228
Tequila, 17–18

Tequila-based drinks, 128–29, 132–33, 188, 191, 209, 212, 223–32
Tequila Collins, 228
Tequila Fizz, 229
Tequila Mano, 229
Tequila Old-Fashioned, 230
Tequila Rickey, 230
Tequila Sour, 231
Tequila Sunrise, 231
Tequonic, 232
Triple Sec, 119
Tropical Freeze, 194
Tropical Mojito, 194
Turkish Harem Cooler, 162
Twister, 240

V

Vanilla Orange Smoothie, 195
Vegetable juices, 20
VeryBerrytini, 266
Vodka, 18, 267–68
Vodka and Tonic, 240
Vodka-based drinks, 128, 130–31, 187, 190, 192–93, 195, 212, 233–41, 257–62, 264–66
Vodka Collins, 241

W, X, Z

Washington, 182
Watermelon Slushie, 195
Watermelontini, 266
W.C.T.U., 183
Weight loss, 274
Weissbeer Mojito, 93
Westminster, 173

Whiskey, 15
    Scotch Honey Whiskey, 117
    Southern Whiskey, 118
Whiskey and Cola, 253
Whiskey-based drinks, 186, 210–11, 210–11, 243–53
Whiskey Cooler, 253
White Cobbler, 163
White Flame, 163
White Wine Spritzer, 164
Wine-based drinks, 155–64
Wine openers, 4
Wines
    carbohydrate counts of, 135–53, 268, 275
    stocking, 26
Worcestershire Sauce, 22
XYZ Cocktail, 133
Zoom, 183

About the Author

Bob Skilnik is a Chicagoland freelance writer who frequently writes for the *Chicago Tribune* and the American Breweriana Association's *Journal* magazine. His articles on beer, brewing, breweriana, and brewery history have been included in the *Collector Magazine* and the National Association [of] Breweriana Advertising's *Breweriana Collector*. He is a 1991 graduate of the Chicago-based Siebel Institute of Technology, the oldest brewing school in the United States, with a degree in Brewing Technology.

His interests in beer and brewing were cultivated while serving as a German translator in West Germany for the United States Army. Skilnik is an associate editor for the American Breweriana Association's *Journal* and *The Tap* newspaper in Chicago where he also writes a monthly column about beer. He has appeared on television and radio throughout the United States and Canada, including WOR's *Morning Show* with Ed Walsh in New York, SD's *Talk Radio Gourmet Club*, ESPN2's *Cold Pizza*, and *FOX News Live*. Skilnik also pens a bimonthly column ("The Low-Carb Bartender") for *Low Carb Energy Magazine*.

Skilnik's first book, *The History of Beer and Brewing in Chicago, 1833–1978*, was published in 1999. The book was awarded the Quill & Tankard Award by the North American Beer Writers Guild (NABWG) as "Best Beer Book" of 1999. *The Low-Carb Bartender* is his fourth book.